STUDIES IN COMPARATIVE POLITICS

The purpose of the collection 'Studies in Comparative Politics' is to provide the students of politics with a series of up-to-date, short and accessible surveys of the progress of the discipline, its changing theoretical approaches and its methodological reappraisals.

The format of the individual volumes is understandably similar. All authors examine the subject by way of a critical survey of the literature on the respective subject, thus providing the reader with an up-to-date *bibliographie raisonnée* (either separate or contained in the text). Each author then proposes his own views on the future orientation. The style tries to bridge the often lamented gap between the highly specialised language of modern political science and the general reader. It is hoped that the entire collection will be of help to the students who try to acquaint themselves with the scholarly perspectives of contemporary politics.

S. E. Finer
Ghiţa Ionescu

Already published
C. H. DODD : Political Development
GHIŢA IONESCU : Comparative Communist Politics
DENNIS KAVANAGH : Political Culture
LESLIE J. MACFARLANE : Political Disobedience
W. J. M. MACKENZIE : The Study of Political Science Today
WILLIAM WALLACE : Foreign Policy and the Political Process
ROGER WILLIAMS : Politics and Technology
LESLIE WOLF-PHILLIPS : Comparative Constitutions

Forthcoming titles
A. H. BROWN : Soviet Politics and Political Science
BERNARD CRICK : Elementary Types of Government
S. E. FINER : The Study of Interest Groups
GEOFFREY K. ROBERTS : What is Comparative Politics?

STUDIES IN COMPARATIVE POLITICS

published in association with

GOVERNMENT AND OPPOSITION

a quarterly journal of comparative politics, published by Government and Opposition Ltd, London School of Economics and Political Science, Houghton Street, London, WC2A 2AE.

Political Culture

DENNIS KAVANAGH

Lecturer in Government, University of Manchester

Macmillan

First published 1972 by

THE MACMILLAN PRESS LTD
London and Basingstoke
Associated companies in New York Toronto
Dublin Melbourne Johannesburg and Madras

SBN 333 13749 3

Printed in Great Britain by
THE ANCHOR PRESS LTD
Tiptree, Essex

292267
6001001450   Cd

CONTENTS

Preface   7

1 Approaches to Political Culture   9

2 Subcultures   20

3 Political Socialisation   28

4 Political Culture and Change   37

5 On Problems of Method and Comparison   49

6 Problems and Shortcomings   55

References   70

Select Bibliography   79

PREFACE

In the scope of this short essay I have not tried to deal exhaustively with the large subject of political culture. Instead, I have tried to analyse critically as well as to review substantively the major studies according to a number of themes. In the first two sections I examine the ways in which political scientists have handled the subjects of political culture and political subcultures. In the next two sections I examine the sources of the political culture and the ways in which it changes. The final two sections are more methodological in their emphasis: in one I examine the problems involved in the study and comparative analysis of political cultures; in the other I try to pinpoint the shortcomings found in much of the work.

D. K.

1. APPROACHES TO POLITICAL CULTURE

The subjective aspects of politics have long been a legitimate interest to students of government. Bagehot and de Tocqueville are still read as seminal works on the important role played by values, sentiment and symbols in British, French and American politics. Rousseau, or even Plato before him, attached great importance to the inculcation of public sentiments appropriate to political democracy. Dicey, of course, traced the emergence of collectivist legislation in late Victorian England and attributed it to changes in the public mood concerning the role of government. More recently, Louis Hartz has argued that the absence of feudal tradition in the United States has led to a 'Lockean consensus' around liberal values, and that the absence of class-consciousness and overt symbols of hierarchy in America has hampered the development of conservative and socialist parties along European lines.[1]

Such writings, however, insightful as they sometimes were, often suffered from being essentially impressionistic. That they are no longer fashionable is, I would suggest, one of the more rewarding consequences of the behavioural impact of political studies.[2] The subjective aspects are now amply covered in the rich and burgeoning literature on political culture. In part this change has been a consequence of the development of tools and techniques of data-gathering and analysis, particularly in the field of survey research, and advances in anthropology and psychology. In part also it has been a reaction to the speculative and impressionistic basis of much of the traditional work in this field, and to the legal-institutional study of politics which often implied that political actors and institutions actually behaved along lines prescribed by constitutional forms. The modern concern to present evidence which has been collected and analysed according to accepted canons of scientific research has enhanced our ability to make more precise characterisations of a population's psycho-cultural orientations to politics, and also increased the possibilities of making more genuine cross-national comparisons across political cultures.

Definitions of political culture are many and varied. Roy Macridis writes of it as the 'commonly shared goals and commonly accepted rules'.[3] Samuel Beer made the concept of one of four variables crucial to the analysis of political systems. According to Beer, the components of the culture are values, beliefs, and emotional attitudes about *how* government ought to be conducted and about *what* it should do.[4] Robert Dahl has singled out political culture as a factor explaining different patterns of political opposition.[5] The salient elements of the culture for Dahl are :

1. Orientations of problem-solving; are they pragmatic or rationalistic?
2. Orientations to collective action; are they co-operative or non-co-operative?
3. Orientations to the political system; are they allegiant or alienated?
4. Orientations to other people; are they trustful or mistrustful?

Lucian Pye has been particularly concerned with the aspects of political culture pertaining to political development in the new states. For Pye the indicators of a nation's political culture include such factors as : the scope of politics; how ends and means in politics are related; the standards for the evaluation of political action; the values that are salient for political action.[6] Finer's definition of a nation's political culture seems to concentrate largely on the legitimacy of the rulers and political institutions and procedures.[7]

For our purpose we may regard the political culture as a short-hand expression to denote the emotional and attitudinal environment within which the political system operates. It is the 'particular pattern of orientations' in which, according to Gabriel Almond, every political system is embedded.[8] Borrowing from Talcott Parsons,[9] we can be a little more precise at this point, and say that we are concerned with *orientations* towards *political ob-*

10

jects. Orientations are predispositions to political action and are determined by such factors as traditions, historical memories, motives, norms, emotions and symbols. We can break down these orientations into their component parts as follows: cognitions (knowledge and awareness of the political system); affect (emotional disposition to the system); and evaluation (judgement about the system). Political objects include such parts of the political system as the executive, legislature and judiciary, the political parties and pressure-groups, the individual's view of himself as a political actor, and his views of other citizens.

The political culture, then, may be seen as the overall distribution of citizens' orientations to political objects. Such a mode of analysis, though largely derivative from Parsons and not without shortcomings, represents a considerable advance on previous global descriptions of such phenomena as a nation's 'political character'. We are now encouraged to think in terms of *what* kind of orientations are held by *which* people towards *which* political objects. For example, recent research on popular attitudes to the Federal German Republic found a high degree of awareness and information about the democratic institutions, but a much lower degree of emotional commitment to them.[10] Almond and Verba have cleverly drawn on the cognitive, affective and evaluative dimensions of attitudes about the political objects to develop a typology of *ideal* political cultures, participant, subject and parochial.[11] Where orientations are positive to all the objects, they suggest that the political culture is *participant*; the British, American and Scandinavian political systems best represent this ideal. Where the citizens assume a passive or obedient relationship to the system, perceiving themselves as hardly affecting the system, though being affected by it, they regard the political culture as a *subject* one; the East European and many new states approximate this type. Finally, where the individual hardly relates himself to the political system at all and has only a dim awareness and knowledge of it, they classify the political culture as *parochial*; this type is found in many traditional societies. It is worth stressing that these are ideal-types. In point of fact there are invariably mixes of these outlooks within any political system and also within individuals. Only about a quarter of British adults meet criteria for the above pure types.[12]

11

The political culture is but a part of the larger culture of a society. In a sense it is a subculture, influenced by the general culture. In France, the widespread popular distrust of the government has been related to the low levels of interpersonal trust in French social relations. In Britain, accommodative personal relationships seem to parallel a broadly allegiant posture to government. Later we shall discuss in more detail the relationships between the two cultures.

Broadly speaking, the tendency of political scientists trying to explain the nature and performance of political systems has been to emphasise cultural and/or structural factors. For example, a frequently canvassed explanation of Germany's inability (until recently) to operate democratic institutions stressed the anti-democratic consequences of the authoritarian family structure in Germany.[13] This psychological emphasis ignored the fact that families in several other European states at this time were dominated by authoritarian father-figures without this producing an Adolf Hitler. Structuralists, on the other hand, have argued that there are certain economic and social prerequisites for sustaining stable democracy. Another group, the institutionalists, has emphasised the influence of political rules, e.g. the role of a constitution or of the electoral system, in determining the nature of the party system.

The chequered histories in this century of France and Germany are inconvenient exceptions to the theory positing economic and industrial prerequisites for democracy, and the unhappy history of the Weimar Republic and the short life-span of Westminster-type constitutions exported to African states underline the significance of the values and motives of the people working the institution. Marxists would tend to argue, of course, that ideas and emotions together with the political institutions are *merely* the consequences of class relationships and the economic structure. Clearly, a rich explanation of political phenomena will draw on both cultural and structural factors. For heuristic purposes, however, there is something to be said for singling out one or other of the approaches. An interesting case here is the work of Max Weber on the connection between Protestant values and the rise of capitalism. Though primarily concerned to evaluate the contribution of the Protestant ethic to capitalism, Weber did not exclude the

12

influence of other factors. He stated: 'We only wish to ascertain whether and to what extent religious forces have taken part in the qualitative and quantitative expansion of that [capitalistic spirit] over the world.'[14]

It is worth tapping the political culture for two reasons. One is that the citizens' attitudes to the political system clearly affect the kinds of demands made, the way they are expressed, the response of the elites, the reserves of popular support for the regime – in sum, the orientations which condition the performance of the political system. According to a recent study:

> The kinds of orientations which exist in a population will have a significant influence on the ways in which the political system works. The demands made upon the system, the responses to laws and appeals for support, and the conduct of individuals in their political roles, will all be shaped by the common orientation patterns.[15]

The political culture approach enhances our ability to describe and analyse the interactions between the political system and its culture. By distinguishing between behaviour and attitudes, we are able to explicate differences in performance across political systems and structures in terms of the culture.

A second reason is that, by understanding the nature of the relationship between the political culture and the system's performance, we are better able to appreciate means by which progressive political changes might be brought about. This is particularly relevant to the many political scientists engaged in locating the conditions of stable democratic government.

Having established what political culture is and its importance to students of politics, we are confronted with a further question, namely, what to do with it? The political culture is, of course, an analytical abstraction; i.e. we abstract information from the larger environment about the knowledge, feelings and evaluations of people to their politics. Moreover, we are talking about the predispositions which give shape and meaning to political acts; the political culture does not *do* anything. As a mediating rather than a determining influence, the concept of political culture helps us to explain why broadly similar phenomena across nations

13

produce dissimilar results, e.g. why the working-class movement in Britain took more allegiant forms than it did on the Continent. Rather than being able to make predictions about the future performance of a political system, we are sensitised to the limits of popular understanding and support within which it is likely to operate. It is worth stressing that we must beware of making inferences from predispositions to actual behaviour. Some attitudes are more actionable than others : attitude-holders vary both in the intensity of their beliefs and in their willingness to act on them; and, depending on the issue and the person concerned, the structural possibilities for action also differ. For example, some three-quarters of Britons and Americans believe themselves capable of influencing their government, though only small proportions have actually tried to exercise such influence.

At times, however, this concentration on the psychological to the exclusion of action or behavioural variables involves severe disadvantages. Richard Fagen found that such an emphasis was of little help in his study of the transformation of Cuban political culture.[16] The Cuban political leadership was concerned to change not only the attitudes but also the manifest political behaviour of the masses; the leaders' vision of the new political culture consisted of transformed political values as well as political behaviour. Fagen therefore required an approach which encompassed behavioural as well as attitudinal factors.

If political scientists now tend to be more cautious in their delineation of a nation's political culture, they have not relaxed their claims for its explanatory power. Almond and Verba justified their undertaking of a five-nation study on the grounds of its usefulness in explaining the structural-functional characteristics of the political systems under review. Emerging from their research was a theory of the 'civic culture' thought to be most conducive to a stable democracy. This 'civic culture' is a dualistic orientation to political authority, a balance of directive and acquiescent, participant and passive attitudes. It is a mixed political culture in which the subject orientations allow the elites the necessary initiative and freedom to take decisions and are countered by the participant orientations which make the elites sensitive to popular preferences. Looking at the five countries in the light of their resemblance to the 'civic culture' model, they

14

suggest that Britain and the United States best achieve balances of the passive and participant outlooks. However, whereas the bias in the British culture inclines slightly to the passive or deferential, this quality is slightly less entrenched in the United States. The distrust of government in America is linked by the authors to the immobilism which periodically beset that country's political system. The deference-inclined mix in Britain is linked by Almond and Verba to that country's apparently strong and effective government. Among Italians, the authors discern widespread alienation, both as participants and as subjects, from the political system. In Mexico, citizens are often alienated from the policies and institutions of the government but there is loyalty to the system because of its identification with the emotive symbol of the Mexican revolution. These attitudes are linked by the authors with the cynicism and dissatisfaction of many Mexicans with present-day politics and their hopes and expectations that things will get better in the future. In Germany, the subject political outlook has not been matched by a set of participant attitudes which would result in a 'civic culture' mix. Germans tend to be loyal to the outputs of government more than to the system itself, and see their political participation as being rather formal and passive, e.g. voting, rather than informal, e,g, forming political groups and talking about politics. In addition, satisfaction with the performance and rewards of the governments is not matched by loyalty to the system itself. Almond and Verba suggest on the basis of these data that the reserves of unconditional support which the Federal German Republic might call on in a crisis are rather low.

Eckstein's *Theory of Stable Democracy* singles out the importance of authority relations, particularly the degree of harmony between a nation's governmental and social structures, in maintaining stable democracy.[17] According to Eckstein it is the social structures, such as the family and the school, and the political structures, such as parties and pressure-groups which are 'adjacent' to the government, which prepare individuals for governmental roles. Congruence between governmental and other structures reduces strains and brings about appropriate expectations for future roles.

Finer has related the levels of a nation's political culture to the

15

likelihood of its being subject to a military *coup* and also to the methods by which this would come about.[18] The postulated relationship between the culture and the other two factors is set out in Table 1.

Table 1

Level of political culture	Likelihood of coup	Method
Mature	1	Influence
Developed	2	'Blackmail'
Low	3	Displacement
Minimal	4	Supplement

Research has also been conducted into the social and psychological bases of economic and political development. The work of David McClelland on rates of economic growth is particularly concerned with the kind of values which are transmitted to children; his own hypothesis is that the greater the achievement-needs implanted in children (for instance in their reading), the greater the economic growth that will result when the children mature.[19]

Empathy, or the ability of people to relate to one another, has been singled out by Daniel Lerner as a major psychological base for the support of complex structures and associations which we associate with a developed system.[20] Members of traditional societies are often unwilling to identify beyond members of their immediate kinship circle. According to Lerner, the processes of industrialism and urbanism, particularly the greater exposure to the mass media, break down this traditionalism and broaden their outlooks.

Lucian Pye has dealt with the further question as to whether the broader perspective actually enables people to work together.[21] For this to happen, according to Pye, the empathy must be coupled with associational sentiments and skills which can sustain organisations.

Several scholars have focused on attitudes to authority, an undoubtedly important aspect of political culture. Indeed, Peter Nettl defined the political culture as 'the pattern or patterns of knowledge, evaluation, and communications relating to political authority'.[22] Studies of political socialisation have tended to concentrate on the young child's first encounter with

16

such authority-figures as the father, teacher and policeman, and the transfer of these attitudes to the head of state, which is invariably the earliest symbol of the regime to the child. The problem of authority has also loomed large for theorists of political development; many would argue that a fusion of traditional and modern attitudes to political authority is essential for a stable and integrated political culture, as well as easing the transition to political modernisation.

An ambitious attempt to explain democratic stability and instability in terms of authority relations has been made by Eric Nordlinger. The authority dimension of the political culture, according to Nordlinger, is 'a powerful explanatory variable in accounting for the stability, effectiveness, and representativeness of democratic systems'.[23] The plausibility of the theory is defended on two grounds. Firstly, the attitudes to authority held by both elites and voters determine how the government perceives the balance between its twin tasks of leadership and representation; imbalance can result in a government being indecisive and trying to tack its sails to catch each electoral wind, or in a government disregarding popular preference. Secondly, the authority dimension is so central to a country's political culture that one may subsume other factors under it. I have a number of reservations about this theory and will present them later. However, let us first look at Nordlinger's theory with reference to a stable democracy, England, and an unstable one, France.

Nordlinger's own research shows that many English workers possess the favoured dualism of attitudes to authority. The widespread popular acceptance of the independent authority of the government is combined with the belief that the government should be responsive to the electors. Moreover, this mixed outlook is found across social classes and among supporters of both the Labour and Conservative parties. For example, Nordlinger found that approximately half of the working-class supporters of both parties were prepared to accept the decisions of a government regardless of whether or not the government was supported by a popular majority. Equal proportions would also disapprove of the government acting contrary to the wishes of the majority. Among workers who believe themselves to have no influence on government, nearly two-thirds were dissatisfied, and of those who

17

felt themselves having only 'a little influence' on government, two-thirds thought this modest role appropriate. According to Nordlinger, these data show 'an approximate balance' between, on the one hand, workers with directive attitudes towards political authority who believe they should exercise more influence, and, on the other hand, workers with acquiescent attitudes who are content with their passive states.

In France, on the other hand, we appear to be faced with a very different set of attitudes to political authority.[24] The conventional view of the French political culture is that an absolutist conception of authority prevails. The rivalry between the two subcultures of the political right, committed to principles of order and hierarchy, and of the political left, committed to principles of change and equality, means that the values of autonomous leadership and popular control of the government are not blended within individuals.[25] Instead, each subculture is only prepared to trust the government when its party is in office. Nordlinger has also drawn on Crozier's work to show how the French avoidance of intimate relations between power-holders and subordinates has been a factor encouraging a centralisation of authority. *L'horreur du face-à-face* has resulted in a concentration of authority in officials and institutions remote from the subjects affected. Only by this centralisation, it is suggested, can the French citizen reconcile (*a*) his acknowledgement of the need for firm leadership with (*b*) his wish to remain free from the dictates of immediate superiors.

Crozier, Nordlinger and a host of other writers on French politics broadly agree that 'such absolutist conceptions of authority' are dysfunctional for the political system. Individuals are often isolated from the political institutions and there tends to be little informal contact between different strata of the elites; a result of what Nicholas Wahl calls 'this cultural schizophrenia' has been discontinuity between regimes of order and of movement.[26] Hostility to government has tended to end in bouts of *immobilisme* and periodic crises, which are only liquidated by extraordinary grants of power to remote arbiters like de Gaulle and Pétain.

A second effort to develop an empirical theory of stable democracy which draws on the authority variable is Eckstein's 'congruence' hypothesis, which we have already noted.[27] Eckstein

18

suggests that prospects for stability will be increased where there are 'graduated resemblances' between the socio-political and the governmental relationships. Authority patterns widely divergent from those in government are tolerable as long as they are confined to spheres which are remote from the government. A large part of Britain's political stability is explained, for Eckstein, by the deferential norms which dominate political as well as social relationships. The expectation that the British executive will govern decisively, even in the face of unpopularity, is paralleled by hierarchic relations between party leaders and their backbenchers, and this in turn closely approximates the kind of behaviour found in the public schools and in the upper-class families which are most likely to provide recruits for government. On the other hand, the instability of the Weimar regime is related by Eckstein to the wide gap between the democratic rules for the conduct of government and the authoritarianism found in the military, the bureaucracy, the political parties and the family. Eckstein suggests that a major reason for the instability of the Weimar Republic was that it imposed parliamentary democracy on an authoritarian society. The prospect for stability would presumably have been enhanced had more links with the pre-1918 authoritarian system been retained.

2. SUBCULTURES

A nation's political culture is really a metaphor, and may conceal marked variations in the orientations to politics of different groups of the population. The term is probably as amorphous as 'public opinion'; in reality we should speak of the opinions of sections of the public. These different group orientations, which may or may not result in an integrated and coherent culture, we call 'subcultures'. This is a useful term, for it enables us to break up large generalisations and to observe deviations from 'expected' behaviour. Heinz Eulau has shrewdly suggested that it is probably best for us to think of an aggregate of subcultures rather than of 'whole' cultures.[28] Region, religion, social class, language, generation and occupation are often basic reference-groups for many people and provide the important cleavages in political systems. In addition, there are role-cultures, arising from the orientations commonly associated with one's position in the political system, e.g. in the bureaucracy, political party or interest-group.

Some of these subcultures are described below.

ELITE VERSUS MASS CULTURES

In Britain and America there are ample data to suggest that the democratic political culture, i.e. understanding of an approval for liberal-democratic principles, is concentrated among the political elite, activists and opinion-leaders.[29] Culture gaps between political leaders and masses are also found in Ceylon[30] and India. The political leaders in these countries have often been trained in foreign schools and adopted foreign ways, and are much more metropolitan and cosmopolitan in their outlooks than the voters. Indeed, Weiner has felt able to identify two political cultures in India:[31] an elite one which is secular, modern and national, and a mass one in which orientations are particularistic, emotional and populist.

The opportunities and constraints provided by the institutional-cultural matrix in which political leaders operate condition the style in which the political elite performs. In British politics, recruitment patterns, particularly the conventions that would-be leaders serve long apprenticeships in the political party and in Parliament, combined with the cabinet system of government, have diminished the opportunities for a heroic style of leadership. In France, on the other hand, Hoffmann has convincingly written of such a leadership style, shared by Pétain, Mendès-France and de Gaulle, which has been the usual method of liquidating crises, following the *immobilisme* in the National Assembly.[32] In a role-culture such as the civil service Weber has introduced us to certain norms and values of the bureaucratic ethos, often induced by the skill requisites, traditions, recruitment processes and the institutions themselves. Studies of a legislature, be it the American Congress or the French National Assembly, invariably emphasise the conventions and 'rules of the game' which constitute its 'culture'. Under the Fourth Republic, deputies were sometimes so absorbed in the game of making and unmaking cabinets that they easily lost touch with the world outside Parliament; to some observers the National Assembly became a 'house without windows'.[33]

GENERATIONS

Rapid social transformation invariably highlights the culture gaps between generations. Almond and Verba showed how, across their five nations, social and economic change was leading to more participant orientations among younger citizens. In many new states young people are particularly sensitive to appeals based on a political religion. Frequently it is the young, relatively unsullied by direct contact with colonial and traditional values, who are the prime objects of the regime's efforts to create a new culture. The results tend to involve a discontinuity in the values and outlooks *between* generations.

DIVISIONS WITHIN ELITES

Lucian Pye has pointed to the differences in outlooks between Burmese administrators and Burmese politicians.[34] Administrators

21

were frequently trained for a career in a colonial civil service, under British guidance. Their identification with British ways and their respect for orderly and predictable procedures in government have brought them into conflict with the politicians. The latter, recruited through enthusiastic and anti-British national movements, tend to be more emotional and idealistic, and suspicious of the administrators' connection with the British. What emerges, according to Pye, is a fragmented political culture at the elite level, preventing the two groups from reaching a mutual understanding of their roles and hampering the development of a stable sense of Burmese identity. Instead of performing specialised but complementary functions, each group claims exclusive monopoly of the political process.[35]

POLITICAL PARTIES

Parties differ in the emphasis which they place on socialising or integrating the voter into a set of values. In the communist states of East Europe and in many Afro-Asian states, the party, as mobiliser, has a strong ideological bent. Parties in the industrialised Western states are more concerned to represent the various groups than to maintain their ideological purity.

Supporters of competing American and British political parties differ over certain political issues while agreeing on the acceptability of the major institutions. Even here, however, talk of policy subcultures may be exaggerated. It is clear that most voters lack the mental equipment and awareness of politics to interpret political issues along ideological or even party lines.[36] In spite of the parties' ability to maintain the electoral allegiance of most voters, the instability of opinions and high rates of disagreement on policy preference between supporters of a party suggest that party is a rather weak influence on policy outlooks. Also, in Britain and America participant and acquiescent outlooks are distributed across voters with little reference to party.[37] On the other hand, communist and religious parties in France and Italy represent more distinctive subcultures; partisanship between party supporters is intense and pervades family relationships.[38] Supporters of the Italian Christian Democratic Party view with great displeasure the prospect of a son or daughter marrying a socialist or communist; this is not surprising, perhaps, since, in the past, the Vatican has denounced voting for such parties as a sin.

Some cleavages are of more political significance than others. Most important perhaps is loyalty to the nation, 'the major constituting factor of a new nation',[39] according to Verba. As shown in the politics of Northern Ireland, Nigeria and Pakistan in recent years, this question of identification with the national community overrides other divisions. Indeed, apologists for the suppression of dissent in many new states and the phenomenon of one-party regimes argue that these are necessary tactics for integrating the nation; subcultures based on caste, tribe, religion or region are seen as major threats to the integrity of state boundaries and national identity.

Here the way in which decisive episodes in a nation's history have occurred and been managed has long-run consequences for the nature of contemporary subcultures. Did basic questions affecting national identity, church–state relations, workers' demands for welfare and representation, coincide or occur singly? How have elites responded to demands – by accommodation or repression? Are these major historical experiences divisive or unifying reference-points for citizens? Italy and France provide two notorious examples of how it is possible for significant aspects of the state- and nation-building process to be mishandled. In Italy, national integration was achieved by means of Piedmontese arms and at the cost of alienating the Catholic Church; as a result, the church, a major power and source of legitimacy in Italy, for long adopted an antagonistic stance to the secular state. In addition, the integration of the neglected and resentful population in the south still remains a challenge one century later.[40]

In Italy, as in Germany, the workers' party came under Marxist influence from the early days. But in both countries the nonresponsiveness of the elites encouraged the parties of the left to assume a millennial and alienated stance. In Italy, the integration of the communist and socialist parties within 'the system' is still to be achieved. Contrast this with Britain where the rise of the Labour Party was handled in a more conciliatory manner by the elites; a consequence in part of this responsiveness was that party's commitment to parliamentary institutions and an expectation that reformist methods would bring about desired changes.

Efforts have been made to specify the conditions in which the inevitable divisions in the culture will weaken the performance of the political system even to the point of threatening its stability. For example, Gabriel Almond, in a seminal paper, has explained the greater political stability of Britain and America over France and Italy in terms of the differences in the subcultures between the two pairs of countries.[41]

In Britain and America, according to this analysis, the political culture is homogeneous, in that most citizens have shared or fused different values; role-structure such as parties, pressure-groups and the communications media are relatively autonomous; and individuals belong to a variety of overlapping groups. The result has been that politics is conducted in a bargaining or secular spirit, that citizens tolerate different loyalties and identities, and that role-structures are differentiated. In France and Italy, on the other hand, the culture has been fragmented into contradictory subcultures which are embedded in the various structures. Moreover, group loyalties tend to reinforce or parallel each other; for instance, Catholics will vote for Catholic-oriented parties, belong to Catholic labour unions, read Catholic papers, and tend to restrict close friendships to fellow Catholics. Such highly partisan attachments to groups affect interest-groups, parties and the media, which are inevitably hampered in their specialist roles of converting demands into bargainable policy alternatives. The mutual reinforcements of social, religious and political loyalties increase antagonism between subcultures. I am less concerned at this point with the political consequences alleged to follow from the culture than with the way in which Almond perceives the overall qualities of homogeneity, fragmentation and pragmatism-rigidity as stemming from the subcultures.

His argument is, of course, very similar to that of the pluralist theory of democracy. A salient feature of this thesis is that cross-cutting cleavages and subcultures moderate partisanship and thereby underpin the stability of the system.[42] Much of this analysis, like that of Almond, has been drawn from observation and comparison of Anglo-American democracies with Continental European countries.

However, the smaller European democracies – for example,

24

the Netherlands, Switzerland and Belgium – are significant deviations from the theory. These countries possess mutually antagonistic subcultures without their political stability being imperilled. For example, the Netherlands is a strongly segmented (*verzuiling*) society, consisting of three well-entrenched subcultures, Catholic, Calvinist and secular.[43] For the majority of citizens party loyalty is associated with membership of the 'appropriate' trade union, church, recreational group, schooling and newspaper exposure. In terms of the distribution and intensity of attitudes, one is tempted to think of the Netherlands as 'several nations inhabiting the same country'. According to Arend Lijphart, the reason for the greater stability in the Netherlands, compared with France and Italy, lies in the fact that the Dutch political system is a *consociational* democracy,[44] so called because the elites in Parliament are willing and able to compromise and co-operate with one another in spite of the isolation of the subcultures at the mass level; in other words, antagonistic subcultures are not fatal for political stability where the political elites fail to transmit to government the bitterness felt at the mass level. In contrast with Italy and France, where the political elites have often been unable or unwilling to bridge the gap, the commitment of elites in the Netherlands to maintaining the system has prevented the cleavages from paralysing the government.

Some of the conditions suggested by Lijphart, in which fragmentation and contradictions in the political culture will permit the emergence of the stabilising form of consociational leadership, are set out below.[45] At the level of the elites, it is likely to emerge where:

1. The elites recognise the dangers of cultural fragmentation to the integrity of the state or to other desirable goals. For example, the willingness, until recently, of the major parties in Austria to form a grand coalition since 1945 has in part resulted from the learning experience of the unfortunate consequences which attended the failure to arrive at such an accommodation in the inter-war years.
2. The elites are committed to the maintenance of the system.
3. The elites accept the need for accommodation, and are skilful enough to bring it about.

4. The elites grant proportionality of rewards and vetos on sensitive issues to the groups. In the Netherlands, government subsidies and appointments to the cabinet are distributed between groups. Other 'rules of the game' which help the elites to bargain are the emphasis on secrecy and the tendency to depoliticise issues.

Conditions found in the social structure and mass culture which encourage competing elites to come together are :

1. Where there is low loading on the system. Ideally, major issues should be handled singly. In modern British politics the outstanding failure in peacefully resolving conflict was the Irish question between 1914 and 1921. Here, divisions between North and South were made insoluble by traditional incremental and bargaining methods because the very cumulativeness of subcultural ties made the parties more implacable. Religion and national identity were both involved and were mutually reinforcing divisions.
2. Where there is an approximate balance of power between groups, providing incentives for them to co-operate with each other. In the Netherlands, no one subculture is in a position to dominate the other two; at the same time no two are close enough to come together and penalise the third. The requirements of government force the parties into a coalition in which they de-emphasise their particular preferences where these provoke strong opposition.
3. Where there are clear divisions and infrequent contacts between the subcultures. It is argued that such isolation reduces the potentially stressful interchanges which might threaten the identity and autonomy of particular subcultures.
4. Where there is deference to political elites. The discretion allowed to party leaders by voters allows bargains and compromises to be made at the elite level.

Other factors influence the relationship between the subcultures and the political system. Particularly important appear to be the bases of the cleavages between parties. Lipset and Rokkan have traced party divisions in modern Europe to the Reformation and the Industrial Revolution, and the parties' institutionalisation of the resultant urban-rural, religious, regional and class divisions.[46] A recent attempt to assess the relevance of these divisions for strains on the regimes of seventeen countries suggested that where parties divide along class lines, regime strains are few.[47] Where, however, parties are based on religious or anti-religious loyalties, then regime strains are high. Economic differences between classes can be settled by bargaining, by welfare and redistributive policies, and by economic growth. Religious divisions, on the other hand, are less amenable to incremental adjustments.

Much also depends on the degree to which the subcultures are institutionalised by the parties. Derek Urwin has argued that in Belgium the representation of class and religious cleavages by the parties has led to the semi-official 'recognition' in the political arena of the claims of such groups, and in turn increased the possibilities for the resolution by political methods of grievances based on class and religion.[48] The non-institutionalisation by the parties of the language issue, however, has left this issue as the major threat to Belgian political stability. According to Val Lorwin, 'there are no recognised representatives qualified to formulate demands, to negotiate, and to fulfil commitments' (apropos the linguistic issue).[49] The failure of this subcultural cleavage to be articulated has hindered the emergence of a comprehensive style of consociational democracy in Belgium.

3. POLITICAL SOCIALISATION

An obvious question is: how does the political culture come to be what it is? What explains differences in the way people across nations think and feel about politics, and why, even within a country, do groups differ? Not the least of our reasons for wanting to understand the causes is that our ability to suggest means for inducing political change and to make probability statements about the future of political systems will be heightened. 'Political socialisation' is the term used to describe the process whereby the individual learns about and develops orientations to politics. The agents of political socialisation are numerous; the family and the school have attracted much of the scholarly research, but a political institution such as a political party, history, outstanding political experiences, occupation, and the educative efforts of the regime are some other agents.

The study of political socialisation has been a major growth area in recent years. However, two caveats are in order concerning the bulk of this vast and still increasing literature. Firstly, much of the discussion has seen socialisation fulfilling a system-maintaining function: stability was 'good' and 'positive' and socialisation was the means whereby the individual became aware of and fitted into the political system and culture. Those who deviated from the culture were often seen as being somehow inadequately socialised. It may well be, however, that the agents usually examined, such as the family and school, in these studies, are primarily 'maintaining' agencies, and that change in the culture results from less studied factors such as policy alterations, wars, economic depressions and political leadership.[50] In fact, there are cases where parents deliberately refuse to pass on their values without this causing political instability; indeed, where there has been an abrupt change between political regimes, the transmission of previously approved or accepted values might be destabilising for the new system. The pre- and post-revolutionary generations in Russia[51] and the pre- and post-war generations in Germany are cases in point of the stabilising consequences of non-replication of values.[52] Moreover, even where the political culture is replicated, it is unlikely to be conducive to stability, peace and orderly life if it is poorly adapted to the new demands on the system. In many transitional societies the basic socialisation process offered in the tradition-bound family ill prepares an individual for the role-demands of a modernising political and social system. The overall effect of the socialisation process, then, may be to change, or even re-create, as well as sustain, the political culture.

Secondly, researchers into political socialisation, perhaps in consequence of a desire to show the 'relevance' of their studies to the political system, have often made highly speculative inferences from data about the orientations of young children to the adult political culture and the likely future performance of the political system.[53] Such inferences involve a large number of connecting links and unproven assumptions about transfers from childhood to political adulthood. The assumptions include: socialisation → personality → political beliefs → individual behaviour → aggregate pattern of behaviour.[54] Moreover, there is also the assumption that these connections are made in predictable ways. As many other experiences and learning agencies intervene between childhood and adulthood, and as socialisation is a developmental process, we can afford to be less deterministic in our view of childhood orientations.

A related example of an inferential fallacy is the tendency to work back from the political system and make assumptions about the nature of the socialisation process which will 'explain' the political system or adult behaviour. The assumption has often been made that the alleged politicisation of French adults is largely inherited from parents. In fact, this is not supported by the available evidence. The Converse–Dupeux survey suggests that only a quarter of French adults were able to report a paternal party preference, whereas Americans were three times as likely to identify such a preference. Recent study of the political orientations of children in Grenoble also shows a low recognition of and attachment to political parties. Inferences from putative

29

features of the British political system and culture (e.g. allegiance, deference, etc.) about the results of the socialisation process are unsupported by recently collected survey data.[55] The data show that schoolchildren, far from sharing the highly deferential and supportive political attitudes expected of them, tend to be quite grudging in their allegiance in comparison with children of other nations.[56]

There are numerous socialising agents, exercising differential influences, and varying in the degree to which they reinforce or contradict each other. In the early years of an individual's life his family plays a major role, but as he attends school, takes up an occupation and generally becomes exposed to peer-group influence, he is being socialised by a gradually increasing and complex number of agencies. Where the agency is primarily non-political, e.g. the family, we may think of it as *latent socialisation*, in contrast with *purposive socialisation* which is expressly designed to affect attitudes.

Interest in the family as a determinant of the culture stems from its primacy and its diffuseness as a socialising agent. Here, for example, is where the potential citizen first becomes aware of power relationships and experiences authority in a broad number of contexts. The studies of voting behaviour show how durable family influence can be. In Britain, the best predictor of a person's vote is not his social class, but how his parents voted. Hyman, drawing mainly on American evidence of a decade ago, has shown the impressive continuity of political outlooks and party preferences between parents and children.[57]

The amount of schooling children receive and their experiences with teachers appear to be a major influence on the development of an individual's sense of political competence.[58] Indeed, the authors of *The Civic Culture* found that when they analysed data by the variables of childhood participation in making school decisions and exposure to higher education, as facilitators of political participation and sense of competence, differences in these qualities across their five nations were significantly reduced. The obvious amenability of schools to political direction has heightened their importance in many new states and in East European communist states engaged in remaking a political culture. Often the result is a challenge to traditional authority patterns

30

in the family : the younger children are socialised into the norms of the new regime more effectively than parents who may retain values associated with an earlier regime. In America, generations of schoolchildren have been the means of 'Americanising' their immigrant parents.

As suggested, we should be cautious in assuming a generalisation from experiences in the family to the political system. Although Almond and Verba found that participation in the family, school and work-place correlated with higher levels of political participation, they also argued that transfers from the family to the political system were the least likely in modern industrialised societies. In such states there are more sharply delineated boundaries between society and polity, and more specialised political roles and structures. Experiences at places of work and in voluntary organisations are relevant because they are more contemporaneous with the individual's assumption of citizenship and closer in structure to the political system.[59] The tendency of Germans to compartmentalise political from social life has meant, Verba suggests, a relative failure of democratic sentiments fostered by the latter sphere to be carried over to the former.[60]

Where, however, boundaries between the social and political spheres are poorly defined, then the behaviour and authority patterns found in the family do tend to be transferred. In the Philippines, according to Grossholtz, the political arena and political roles are almost unlimited. Familial behaviour strongly affects expectations about government officials and politicians; politics, like the family, is seen as the provider of basic needs, affecting jobs, health and so on. Life tends to be seen in terms of power relationships; obligations to superiors are accepted on the understanding that the subordinate is able to claim certain rights.[61] In politics the vote is regarded by electors and politicians alike as a *quid pro quo*, given in return for bribes and favours.

But the generalisation of social values to the political sphere is not confined to systems in which the political arena is poorly delimited. Almond and Verba have shown how, in the well-defined politics of Britain and America, an individual's trust in other people affects his political values. Given the remoteness of politics for the vast majority of people even in such relatively 'participant' states as Britain and America, and the dominance of other roles, e.g. spouse, worker, parent, etc., we are justified in assuming the prior importance for political socialisation of attitudes to more salient aspects of society. The Catholic Church in Italy has emphasised the value of submissiveness to lawful authorities, in this case to Catholic priests, teachers and parents, and this has carried over to a generally hostile attitude to the citizen's perception of himself as an autonomous and self-directing actor in the political sphere.[62] Christian Democratic voters tend to be politically dogmatic and socially intolerant in their outlook.[63] Even among politicians, Christian Democrats are the most authoritarian.[64] In Mexico, the generally passive and resigned orientations to the social environment carry over to limit the sense of competence vis-à-vis the political system.

Western political parties are important in giving electoral cues to supporters, more obviously in evaluating policies and leaders. However, they also play a role in colouring values. Even the British Labour Party, long regarded as a classic case of a socialist party being tamed by the dominant culture, did much to promote acceptance of the symbols and values of equality, collectivism and welfare.[65] Historically, the Social Democratic Party in Germany was important in developing solidarity among the working class *against* other groups. The integration of pre-war Social Democratic workers in Germany involved a rejection of the dominant system – a case of *negative integration* into the German political culture.[66] In modern Western industrialised societies, political parties have de-emphasised their ideological orientations; they tend to be much less concerned with their role as a socialising agent and more of a 'catch-all' party, concerned to maximise their electoral followings.[67] This analysis, a variant on the 'end of ideology' refrain, is attributed to the generally homogenising influences of industrialism, urbanism and the mass media. These have, it is suggested, eroded subcultures and forced parties to make nationwide appeals. Some qualification is needed here, however. Ideological politics, based on class, has undoubtedly waned over the past generation. However, the expression of religious, regional and linguistic cultures in politics is still significant.[68]

In the newer states, the party often plays a major role in creating or changing the political culture. Given the relative institutional underdevelopment in such states, the party becomes more than an electoral or aggregating instrument; it is also a supplier of jobs and a means of bringing people into contact with the government, providing information, integrating various groups and propagating national programmes – in short, the task of political socialisation looms large.[69] Indeed, in the developing areas the fact that the parties are often already part of the political culture before political institutions are created heightens this socialising role. In Western states, many of the institutions preceded the development of organised parties.[70]

Symbols are also important means of developing political orientations. Events such as May Day parades, elections, and the anniversaries of Marx and Lenin in the East European countries, the Coronation in Britain and the Presidential inauguration in the United States respectively lay stress on historical continuity and the unity of the nation.[71] In the latter two states the monarchy and the presidency may be significant in that they are the earliest political institutions of which the young child becomes aware, and thus greatly influence the young child's affective and evaluative orientation towards the regime. Positive judgements of the incumbents of these roles precede actual knowledge among children about the President's party affiliation and the Queen's lack of effective powers. It has been speculated that the favourable appraisal of the heads of state in Britain and America carries over to create reserves of support for the regime itself. For Britain, the more full-blown theory of the transfer of affect has been central to the deference stereotype. According to Shils and Eckstein, the traditional domination of government by monarchy and aristocracy has invested their mundane successors with dignity and other deference-evoking qualities. In the absence of development data on attitudes, such a view remains speculative.[72]

Regimes may vary in their exploitation of symbols. In Northern Ireland, religious and historical events provide an armoury of rich symbolism which the Catholic and Protestant communities exploit to maintain existing divisions. The Mexican revolution, on the other hand, has been a potent source of symbolic gratification; it provides many Mexicans with hope and optimism for the future, dulls existing discontents, and generally increases the legitimacy of the present regime. According to Almond and Verba, 'This revolution . . . is the crucial event in the development of the Mexican political culture, for it created a sense of national identity and a commitment to the political system that permeates almost every stratum of society.'[73] That Mexicans display a greater pride in their political and governmental institutions than citizens in the more economically advanced Germany and Italy is traceable in large part to the unifying and legitimising role of the revolution. Castro's revolution in Cuba also appears to have increased favourable system affect in that country.[74]

But the culture is also affected by precursive events as well. Lipset and Rokkan have demonstrated the long-term effects on contemporary party systems and political outlooks of the nature of the social and cultural cleavages existing when the party system was first formed. Parties and their ideologies remain long after the conditions which gave rise to them occurred.[75] In Ireland, the historical absence of a sense of national identity covering the whole country, and the circumstances leading to the 1922 partition, are primary explanations for the cultural fragmentation and divided legitimacy of the Ulster government today.[76] The manner in which the process of state- and nation-building was handled also has long-run consequences for the culture. Particularly apposite here in explaining the contrasts between their political cultures are the different experiences of Britain, Germany and Italy.[77] In England, the consolidation of the central government's authority and the emergence of a central bureaucracy were achieved without obliterating local centres of autonomy and were more conducive to the development of a political culture which has remained relatively participant and pluralist. In Germany, freedom has historically been associated with independence from external powers, not with initiative on the part of citizens. In Germany and Italy, statehood was achieved primarily by the military prowess of Prussia and Piedmont respectively. In Germany, the extreme centralisation of authority and the relatively limited amount of popular participation made the political culture a predominantly *subject* one. In Italy, the manner in which a 'Piedmontised' Italian state was imposed on the Vatican and the south has had lasting and dysfunctional consequences for an integrated Italian political culture. In the south the cul-

34

ture tends to be highly parochial and, overall, alienative aspects figure strongly.

We must not exclude citizens' experiences with the political system itself as a damper or confirmer of values derived from the other sources. Indeed, in many countries governments see the remaking of belief-systems as a major goal. An unfortunate tendency has been to see the political culture as the product of values and influences coming from outside the political system itself. This is implied in Almond and Verba's concentration on the family, school and work-place as causal factors, and political culture and behaviour – e.g. sense of competence and efforts to influence the government – as dependent variables. Although the authors do not exclude experiences with the system itself, this might have loomed larger in their discussion. Wylie's discussion of the French family's influence in implanting mistrust of the government also deals inadequately with the experiences of earlier generations with the political system as a primary cause of the original mistrust.[78] Elsewhere we shall argue that the performance of the system is vitally important in developing citizens' evaluations of it.

Socialisation is a continuous process; it does not stop in childhood or with school. Indeed, it can be argued that overtly political experiences, such as relations with the police and the civil service, and perceptions of politicians and government policies are decisive shaping agents of the political culture because they are more likely to occur in adulthood, at a time when the individual plays a more political role. Moreover, actual experience with governmental institutions and personnel is a 'reality-testing' device for the views taught in childhood. There is a marked decline in the degree of political trust shown by most American children as they mature, in contrast with the almost uniformly positive appraisal and perceptions of the system in childhood. Studies of adults have uncovered cynicism and mistrust. A reasonable speculation is that the origins of some of this mistrust are to be located in later unfavourable experiences with the political culture.

Of course, there can be discontinuities between the influences of the family and other agents. In the Philippines, the schools stress that appointments be made on the basis of merit. This contrasts sharply with the adult political world of vote-buying, tax evasion and nepotism in the allocation of government jobs.[79] Wylie's study

of a village in the Vaucluse has pointed to the incongruities between the positive views of French government presented in the
schools and the cynical sentiments expressed by the parents. In
Britain, on the other hand, it is often held that socialisation experiences are mutually reinforcing and that individuals are prepared
relatively easily for appropriate political roles. Thus working-class
children tend to go to secondary modern schools, take up manual
work, and generally play a subordinate role in society and in
politics. Middle-class children will go to grammar school or public
school, on to university, enter business or a profession, and generally wield authority. From these two groups, political followers and
leaders respectively are drawn. There is a correspondence between
the elite's confidence that the voters will accede to its directions
and the willingness of the latter to defer.[80] In point of fact the
social mobility in Britain is comparable with that of most other
industrialised states, and surveys suggest that many children at
grammar and public schools fail to internalise the suggested
elitist norms, and that secondary modern children often fail to
develop the alleged passive and allegiant attitudes.[81] Again, in
many transitional societies the very diversity and fragmentation
of influences hinders the emergence of shared orientations. Robert
Scott has emphasised that the psycho-cultural shortcomings for
political and social modernisation in Mexico derive from the con-
flicting values and expectations taught by different agents. Although the formal and secondary agents (e.g. schools, political
party) run by the government make people more aware of the
government and its policy outputs, the more tradition-oriented and
suspicious family has slowed down and distorted the transfer of
the above values into a participant outlook. The family is invariably more old-fashioned simply because parents were raised in an
earlier period.[82]

4. POLITICAL CULTURE AND CHANGE

Before examining the major agents of culture change, let us dispense with three widely held misconceptions. Firstly, change is not a process or goal unique to new states. Several societies, possessing well-established national identities, are currently beset by problems of cultural transformation.[83] Russia since 1917, Communist China, Egypt since the overthrow of Farouk in 1952, and post-war Japan and Germany are obvious examples. Each of these states has in common some traumatic experience such as revolution, or defeat in war and enemy occupation, that constituted a break in its history, a rejection of the previous system. However, even a state like Ethiopia, with a strong sense of historical continuity, is experiencing culture change under the pressures to modernise. And Britain, famed for its culture and adaptation, also faces acute culture problems of readjustment to her decline from the status of a world military and economic power.

Secondly, when we refer to the political culture of a society, we are talking about aggregates of individuals. To say that one society is more participant or parochial than another does not mean that all members of the former society are more participant or parochial than members of the latter. We are merely comparing the proportions of individuals with these qualities across the two states. In fact the accelerating rates of political and cultural change today mean that there is great unevenness in the assumption of 'modern' attitudes between individuals within the same state boundaries. Such differential rates in the attainment of modern outlooks tend to be most acute in the developing nations. In addition, describing subjective attitudes about the political system is not tantamount to a realistic description of the system itself. For example, Americans are likely to be much more confident about the opportunities for advancement in their society than are the British or French about theirs; this is not, however, clinching evidence of the degrees of social mobility between the countries. The finding that objective rates of social mobility are similar across the three nations is chastening for those who would make such an inference.[84] Again, the higher frequency of 'participant' or 'democratic' responses made by Americans to survey questions might make the political culture a 'participant' one without this necessarily being true of the political system.

Thirdly, we need to guard against an overly simple view of cultures being *either* traditional *or* modern, the former having a value-system stressing qualities of ascription, particularism and diffuseness, the latter stressing norms of equality or achievement, universalism and specificity. Invariably the values are mixed, within individuals and within the nation. Frank Myers has perceptively objected against F. X. Sutton's division of values into industrial and agricultural, on the grounds that it (a) falsely equates certain values with certain institutions, and (b) assumes that the values are uniformly distributed in the society. In fact such a simple distinction between societies involves a loss of discrimination about differences within industrial societies.[85] In America, for instance, egalitarian values are more concentrated in the middle class, while manual workers tend to develop a compensating 'rationale' for their own failure to achieve high status, and adopt resigned or deferential outlooks.[86] Contrary to the dichotomies suggested by Parsons and Sutton, 'the empirical evidence strengthens the argument that the *logic* of industrialisation is to create different value orientations among different social classes'.[87]

Examination of the Japanese and English political cultures invites consideration of two cultures which show how enduring the traditional quality of deference is in highly industrialised societies. Richard Rose and Robert Ward have stressed the role of the pre-democratic or feudal elements in the political culture in assisting the modernisation process in these two states.[88] Both countries illustrate our observation that states can combine advanced industrialisation and modern political institutions with traditional values. In Britain, according to Rose and others, secularisation of the political culture has not kept pace with the differentiation of the political institutions and the system's capacity for problem-solving. In Japan also, the Meiji dynasty managed to bring about a dramatic technical and industrial transformation while leaving the old values virtually intact.

The political cultures and modernisation experiences of these two states – Britain, the first moderniser; Japan, the only non-Western nation to achieve modernisation – might be of special relevance to leaderships which are trying to bring about similar developments. However, where leaderships are concerned to achieve these changes in a short period, then Japan and Britain show how complex the process can be. In both countries there were long-run antecedents for the changes; moreover, changes were introduced gradually and without violating established values. The resultant blend has made both political cultures 'traditionally modern'. Contrast this with the efforts of many present-day nation-builders who try to create almost *ab novo* and overlook the need to sample the past for those values which may assist the transition to modernisation. A subject political outlook, for instance, may help to contain popular demands while sacrifices and investment for long-term ends can be made. Indeed, the very stability and integration of the political culture depend on promoting orderly changes, and achieving a political consensus depends on the politician's ability to strike a balance between the old and the new. Rajni Kothari is surely right when he points to the conservatising as well as the innovating aspects of political development; ultimately, even innovations in values and institutions are consolidated and legitimated as traditions.[89]

None the less, although a dominant cultural strand has been useful at one point in the modernisation process, it does not follow that it will continue to be so. Again, this depends on the nature of the demands placed on the system. Frank Langdon has argued that the strength of the support attached to the *status quo* and to traditional norms in Japan is now hindering the present and future tasks of political and social modernisation.[90] In particular, the rampant particularism and the submissiveness of the individual to his small group make Diet politics factional, political parties little more than personal followings of the leaders, and hinder the development of national and broad-based parties. In Britain, many of the esteemed deferential traits, the distrust of specialists and the commitment to evolutionary change are now seen by critical observers as a lack of drive, ambition and energy. It is suggested that these qualities reflect themselves in the poor

39

adaptiveness of political institutions, a sluggish rate of economic growth, and in the monopoly of command positions by well-bred and high-status dilettantes. What is needed, according to the critics, is a sharp increase in the norms of egalitarianism and achievement.

Bringing about fundamental changes in the political culture is a major goal of many regimes, and often involves the investment of massive resources. It is true, of course, that the dynamics of social, economic and political development and decay will bring about differing rates of change in components of the political culture. What is interesting about the politics of many new states today, however, is the explicit nature of their efforts to transform the political culture. Few political leaders, committed to speedy industrialisation or political modernisation, are prepared to rely on indigenous values; changes in personality and culture are widely regarded as preconditions of political and socio-economic change. Hence the elaborate endeavours to create the 'new Soviet man' or 'new Cuban man'. In 1965, prior to the Cultural Revolution, Mao stated that 'The thought, culture and customs that brought China to where we found her must disappear. The thought, culture, customs of proletarian China, which does not yet exist, must appear.'

Reconstruction of the political culture looms large in many new states for four major reasons. Firstly, if culture change is to be effected speedily, it will have to be directed by the state – usually by means of secondary and formal agencies. Secondly, the scope of politics is large in such states; society becomes identified with the state, the good man or citizen is the good party man. Thirdly, given the recent discontinuities in the histories of many new states, the creation of new attitudes is important in weakening the pre-revolutionary or pre-independence outlooks. New orientations are necessary to support new institutions and new forms of activity. Finally, the internalisation of regime-approved norms and values is important in strengthening the regime's legitimacy and in encouraging voluntary compliance with its commands.

We have already examined the large number of agents which help create a political culture; they may also help in changing or adapting the culture. Here it is proposed to see how political scientists have handled the question of culture change in its relationship to speeding up political development and/or bringing about democratic stability. This involves elaboration of earlier reference to the debate between those who stress the structural basis of political change and those who emphasise the importance of directly influencing the culture as a necessary precondition of political change. Both views, it will be noted, see politics, particularly political behaviour, as the dependent variable; i.e. it is determined by cultural or structural factors. For example, the belief that social and economic conditions determine values and attitudes and the prospects for stability of pro-American regimes has been a major consideration governing the American foreign aid programme.[91] Alternatively, leaders of many new nations have preferred to concentrate directly on ensuring that members of their societies internalised 'approved' values – via education, harangues, and manipulation of symbols.

In such endeavours, political scientists are emulating anthropologists and psychologists who have concentrated on the subjective determinants of economic growth. For example, David McClelland, following in the footsteps of Weber's thesis on the influence of Protestantism in developing a spirit conducive to capitalism, argues that it is power- or achievement-needs in children, later expressed in entrepreneurial dynamism, inventions and economic growth, which are important. McClelland does not ignore the role of other conditions – climate, skills, opportunities and resources, and so on – but emphasises that the appropriate values and motives must also be present to take advantage of available advantages.

In general, the processes of industrialism and urbanism have been seen as broad instruments of cultural modernisation, where the latter is identified with a participatory outlook. For example, Almond and Verba interpreted the tendency for younger respondents to change in a similar participant direction across the five nations as an aspect of 'the industrialisation, urbanisation, and modernisation processes'. Key features of these processes were a shift from rural to urban residence and from farming to industrial occupations, increased schooling, and the emancipation of women.[92] The Harvard study of the modernisation of attitudes across six developing states has stressed the importance of factory life as a means of promoting active citizenship.[93] Elsewhere,

Almond and Verba specifically single out investment in education as the speediest facilitator of the civic culture. Thus Britain and the United States tended to possess more participants, in large part because they were more industrialised, urbanised and educated than other societies. Lerner has identified exposure to the mass media as the primary agent for bringing about qualities of empathy and other-regardingness.

Using aggregate-statistical techniques, Lipset and Cutright have argued that there are social and economic requisites, in particular a high level of economic development, for stable democracy. Lipset found that states where his indicators of industrialism – communications, urbanisation, education, etc. – were high, were also very likely to be stable democracies. States in which the indicators were low were invariably unstable democracies.[94] Cutright, in a rather similar exercise, tried to establish the degree of correlation between economic development and political development. Both writers felt confident that, on the basis of their researches, they were able to explain democraticness and stable democracy in such structural terms.[95]

Deane Neubauer's sophisticated research has, however, undermined Cutright's claim that a linear relationship exists between economic development and the degree of democracy.[96] According to Cutright, a given increment of the former was associated with an increase in the latter. Neubauer's work, with a sophisticated index of democratic development, suggests that there is a threshold point, above which there is no significant relationship between socio-economic development and degree of democraticness. Values, traditions and patterns of cleavage become important, and exercise an effect independent of socio-economic growth. Neubauer's refinement of the thesis of economic determinism, and his emphasis on the cultural factor, help to explain the significant exceptions like Germany and France to the Lipset–Cutright theory; they also explain why economic development *per se* will not necessarily be associated with significant democratisation in, say, Russia, though it may provide some of the conditions for such an outcome.

Among agents of change in the political culture we might consider the following:

Technological developments in the field of communications have expanded the abilities of leaders to transmit uniform messages from a centralised source to large masses. In many Afro-Asian states the mass media are the major instruments for advancing popular understanding of politics. In addition, they are important in establishing a sense of community among citizens, and in fusing fragmented, parochial and isolative subcultures. In a transitional society the media, in contrast with their role in Western countries, are familiarising people with *new* institutions. 'Hence the mass media are not simply a part of a continuous and coherent training process, as the major socialising agents can be in a stable society, but rather they must be a part of a process of discontinuous change.'[97] Moreover, relative scarcity of communications in such a society decreases the possibilities for selectivity of exposure and perception so often found in the denser communication systems of the West.

As noted, McClelland and Lerner have attached significance to the content of the media in increasing achievement-levels among children and in expanding the psychological perspectives of members of traditional societies. For example, Kemal Atatürk placed radio receivers in remote villages and assisted the speed of literacy by altering the orthography of the Turkish language. Creating the framework for an increased popular exposure to government messages was the major instrument for breaking down traditional values. In Communist China also there has been heavy reliance on the media for establishing a revolutionary culture.[98]

IDEOLOGY

Perhaps the most basic aspect of nation-building is forging a sense of national identity. Many of the new states lack the conventional symbols and traditions of nationhood. One way of eroding tribal and parochial loyalties is to develop a political religion, such as Sukarno's five principles, or Nkrumahism, or by sinking the fragile nation in a larger grouping such as Pan-Africanism or a United Arab Republic. Societies undergoing rapid changes and perplexed as to national identity tend to be most susceptible to political religions. David Apter has suggested several general uses of political religion in the new states: reinforcing the values of

43

hard work and sacrifice; developing a 'collectivity orientation', making citizens aware of their shared ties; developing a political structure; endowing the new order with moral principles; and legitimising the incumbent elite's continual monopoly of office.[99] Apter develops the analogy further : ' . . . the political religion may come to serve as a universal church. Its agents are the missionaries. Opposition to it appears as a new form of imperialism.'[100]

POLITICAL MOBILISATION

The present Cuban and Communist Chinese political leaderships have regarded political participation as the major instrument for destroying the pre-existing cultural fabric. Cultural transformation is to be achieved via political action so that the citizens may actually 'experience' the revolution. In Cuba, Committees for the Defence of the Revolution mobilised the population for demonstrations and ceremonies, distributed scarce resources, instructed the masses in the meaning of the revolution, and assisted in work programmes. As Fagen notes, the Cuban leadership is interested in more than a mere change of attitudes; it wants to transform behaviour as well, and because it sees 'improper behaviour as deriving from corrupt institutional settings and social milieus, environmental reform brings with it the possibility of significant changes in adult behaviour'.[101] Because the lines between the political and the non-political are blurred, the transformation of the political culture is identified with larger changes affecting society itself.

Similar emphases on the totality of the political culture and on transforming the culture and behaviour through participation in the revolution is found in Communist China. According to Mao theory and practice should be united, and the theory of the revolution will only be understood by participation in it, for 'all truths are obtained by direct experience'.[102] Similarly, elections in many new states are often regarded by leaders as occasions for promoting national and political consciousness.

THE POLITICAL PARTY

In mobilisation systems, parties are major instruments of culture change. Parties preaching political religions are what Apter has termed 'parties of solidarity'. Far from being content to act as

44

brokers between groups and individuals, such parties are committed to creating a new normative order, setting socio-political goals, and restructuring existing social relationships. Examples of such parties are seen in many new states and by the communist cadres in Russia.

EXTERNAL INFLUENCES

Revolutions in methods and speed of travel and in communications have undermined the power of geographical boundaries to demarcate national cultures. What happens in one country may have a 'demonstration effect' in a distant one.

A very obvious and, historically, effective way of abetting cultural transformation has been by transfers of populations. The United States, Canada and Australia have in common a 'fragment culture',[103] the result of settlement by British immigrants who imposed their own exported values on the settled country. Again, the American post-war occupation of Japan and the Allied occupations of Germany were examples of the intense application of ideas and values relatively foreign to the native country.

PRIMARY GROUPS

Experiences with the family and school are obvious means of inculcating outlooks which have repercussions for politics. They can, however, be overemphasised as durable influences. Psycho-cultural features of German society (the 'Prussian mentality') have frequently been invoked as explanations for the failure of democratic institutions to take root in that country. After 1945 the West German political leaders determined to democratise social life and thereby democratise the political culture. Almond and Verba show that this experiment in remaking the German political culture has been successful – to a point. Participation in the school and home have indeed increased under the Bonn Republic. However, compared with citizens in other states, Germans transferred participation experiences in primary groups to the political arena less frequently; by the early 1960s, at least, the evidence suggested that the German political culture had been only partly remade. What may be needed for the transfer of primary attitudes to the political orientation may simply be a greater length of time.[104]

Tracing changes in political culture is no simple matter. It has been fashionable for social theorists to see an orderly progress from *Gemeinschaft* to *Gesellschaft* types of societies, or from traditional to modern forms of social relationships. The pattern-variables of Sutton and Parsons used to describe the contrasting role relationships in traditional and modern societies represent an elaboration of this broad distinction, though we have suggested that these should be seen as continuous and not as dichotomous variables. Throughout his work Gabriel Almond has tried to spell out the criteria for a 'developed' political culture. In 1956 he suggested that one should look for qualities of rationality and secularisation, for a culture in which parties, groups and other actors adopted flexible positions and perceived politics as the art of bargaining and arriving at compromises.[105] Borrowing from Parsons's pattern-variables, he has also suggested that political recruitment and rewards should be guided by specialised, achievement-based and universal criteria; family considerations and ties of friendship should be irrelevant. Later, in *The Civic Culture*, of course, the fusion of participant and acquiescent orientations was seen as the desired pattern.[106]

What is perhaps unfortunate is that our concentration on seeking the criteria for distinguishing traditional from modern, and parochial from participant, cultures has encouraged neglect of aspects of 'post-modern' changes. Little effort has so far been devoted to spelling out the criteria for post-modern as opposed to modern political cultures.[107]

To measure the kinds of changes taking place in the political culture, we ideally need longitudinal data. In the case of surveys this presents obvious problems; surveys tend to present snapshots of the political system at one point in time. Panel studies are clearly useful, though generally impossible to maintain for more than a year or so. Converse has suggested that we might reconstruct past orientations by looking at societies at different stages of political and industrial development. An alternative strategy for tracing change is to compare responses across different age-groups. Almond and Verba found that younger generations, across all five nations, tended more often to assume participatory outlooks than did their parents.[108] McKenzie and Silver, comparing the orientations of their different age-groups of working-class Conservatives, showed how deference has been replaced by more instrumental and pragmatic motives for supporting the party.[109] Butler and Stokes divided their massive sample of British voters into four cohorts, according to whether respondents attained adolescence before 1913, during the inter-war years, during the years 1945 to 1950, and, finally, after 1951. This study of 'political generations' proved enlightening in explaining the erosion of the Liberal vote, and the rise of Labour support among the working class.[110] Robert Scott, trying to estimate the displacement of parochial by participant attitudes in Mexico between 1910 and 1960, inferred attitudes to the political input and output structures for the former date, and drew on survey data for the period fifty years after.[111]

Change is not to be equated with *newness*, however. Apparent change may simply be the increased salience in response to political circumstances of previously dormant values. In many Afro-Asian states the emergence of one-party regimes, dedicated to maximising national unity, can be linked to a traditionally consensual style of decision-making at the tribal level. The upsurge in democratic sentiment in Czechoslovakia in 1967–8 becomes less surprising when seen as a rekindling of the traditions of liberalism and parliamentary democracy which had lain dormant since 1948. These traditions singled out Czechoslovakia from the neighbouring communist states along the dimension of political culture.[112]

Speculating about or predicting future patterns of political cultures is bedevilled by two difficulties. One is that criteria of future development are often subjective or qualitative. The other is that 'change' is often confused with terms like 'more democratic', 'participant', 'modern', and so on. Often, predictions of likely change in so complex an area tend to be mere projections of present trends. It is possible, however, to single out from the literature three sets of expectations, each of them usually regarded as cause for optimism.

Firstly, there is the analysis offered by certain observers of the Anglo-American and Scandinavian political systems. They argue that affluence, the softening of divisions between class-based parties, the lessening intensity of partisanship, and general industrial and technological change, have permitted the emergence of political cultures which are more homogeneous and which

47

place increasing stress on bargaining and adaptive qualities. Robert Lane has seen in these changes the means for a greater *rapprochement* between citizen and government. However, such a sanguine expectation must be set against growing fears that industrial societies are tending to develop political and economic structures which are increasing not only in size but also in their impersonality and remoteness.[113] If a political Leviathan is needed to check the powerful corporations, one wonders how this will make ties between voter and government more intimate.

Secondly, there is the possible emergence of a world culture. Lucian Pye has suggested that as citizens of the new states gradually experience industrialism, urbanism and literacy, these common influences will bring about a common culture transcending national boundaries. Differences between nations will no longer be adequately encompassed by terms like 'industrial' and 'non-industrial', 'Western' and 'non-Western', but all national cultures will be seen to be parochial from the world perspective.

Finally, there is the optimism of most scholars that the twin processes of industrialism and urbanism will increase the potential for the diffusion of the participatory outlook in politics. Whether or not the consequences of this outlook are seen as desirable or as a higher stage of development is an open question. The conservative traditions in sociology and politics have related such changes to the emergence of a mass society in which individuals, wrenched from traditional moorings, identities and reference-groups, are alienated, politically impotent, and an easy prey for demagogues who threaten the stability of the polity. Research actually conducted in traditional societies does not entirely support the idyllic portrait penned by Burke, the French romantics and Ortega y Gasset. The findings of Almond and Verba, Banfield, and Lerner suggest in fact that 'traditionals' are often insecure, mistrustful and poorly integrated in society.

5. ON PROBLEMS OF METHOD AND COMPARISON

We have earlier suggested that contemporary studies of political culture tend to present empirically derived evidence in contrast with the traditional methods which relied heavily on intuition, reading and conversation. As Almond and Verba suggest of such studies, 'One questions not merely the interpretations of the facts, but in the first instance the facts themselves.'[114] In addition, the traditional studies were often tautological in their linking of the political culture to the political system. Appraisal of the culture was frequently derived from observation of the institution or behaviour and then used to explain the performance of this same institution or behaviour. Much of the reasoning about the cultural causes and consequences of the British two-party system, or the existence of the monarchy, or the monopoly of high political office by aristocrats, has fallen prey to this kind of circularity. Another fallacy was (and is) to presume that the existence of institutions and procedures was proof of popular commitment to such institutions and values.

We can avoid such risks by adopting certain research strategies. We might infer beliefs *only from some types of political behaviour*, e.g. voting, or attitudes to leaders of differing social status, and use these beliefs to explain *other behaviour*, e.g. compliance with laws. An alternative approach is to infer beliefs from behaviour during a certain time-period and draw on these beliefs to explain behaviour in subsequent periods.[115]

The techniques most commonly used in present analysis of the political culture are survey methods, content-analysis, depth interviews, projective and semi-projective methods, and use of Parsonian pattern-variables. We shall briefly examine each of these in turn.

The Almond and Verba five-nation study has been a landmark in survey research and in comparative politics. As the first direct study of public opinion across nations it has resulted in a dramatic enlargement of empirical data on subjective aspects of the five political systems. Data were collected by means of interviews with approximately a thousand respondents in each of the nations in 1959. It is pointless here to investigate the problems involved in drawing up a questionnaire, locating representative samples, establishing the validity of the instrument – i.e. does it measure what it is supposed to? – and generally establishing a uniform stimulus situation for all respondents. It is enough to say that such difficulties, familiar enough at the national level, were compounded five times for the comparative survey of Almond and Verba.[116] Additional problems were of timing, translation and conducting surveys in traditional areas unfamiliar with such techniques.[117]

In spite of these formidable difficulties the comparative survey offers immense advantages in the study of political culture. Such data present clear advantages in terms of their 'hardness', precision and replicability. Instead of crudely labelling a nation's political culture as 'participant' or 'deferential', we are able to suggest which groups display these features, the intensity of the features, whether they are changing, and, if so, the rate of change.

Less direct is the method of content-analysis. In Cuba, Richard Fagen was not able to conduct survey research after Castro's rise to power.[118] Instead, he chose to study the regime's action programmes which were designed to create 'a new Cuban man'. Fagen focused on the work of two of these programmes – Committees for the Defence of the Revolution, and the Schools of Revolutionary Instruction – relying heavily on methods of content-analysis. David McClelland also employed content-analysis of, for example, children's stories and Greek funeral orations to measure achievement-needs across different societies and different periods. At the level of political elites where data in the form of speeches and writings tend to be rich, content-analysis is a useful means of constructing an individual leader's 'operational code' or the belief-system of a group of leaders.[119] Such an approach is an advance on the old method of gathering facts about the social backgrounds of political elites and then making crude or implicit inferences about their values.

The depth interview, inevitably with small samples, is another available strategy. Robert Lane conducted intensive interviews with sixteen residents in New Haven to collect material on *Political Ideology: Why the American Man Believes What He Does*.[120] Pye's study of political elites in Burma also relied on intensive interviews coupled with Freudian techniques of interpretation. Such approaches, as conducted by Lane and Pye, gain in depth and richness. However, they do pose problems of how representative the sample is of the wider universe. The depth interview would seem more applicable for small groups, e.g. a cabinet or politburo, where the sample can remain small and not lose representativeness, and for suggesting rather than testing hypotheses and insights.

Projective and semi-projective techniques have proved useful in situations where we are exploring the orientations of children to politics, questioning respondents for whom politics is relatively remote, or dealing with potentially sensitive topics. These stimuli situations, because they are less structured than the fixed questions and answers of formal interviews, are more likely to get behind answers which are superficial or simply fabricated by the interviewer's question, and thereby build up a richer picture of the individual's orientations. Greenstein and Tarrow have recently completed a study of children's orientations to their political systems across three nations, relying on semi-projective methods. One of the devices they used to get at images of political leaders was to ask children to complete sentences about incidents describing the head of state being stopped by a policeman for a traffic offence. The children were asked to imagine the conclusion to the incident. McClelland has measured achievement-levels among children by asking them to write stories after being shown blank or ambiguously marked picture cards. The stories were then scored for achievement-need levels.[121]

Seymour Lipset's comparison of political cultures (or 'value-systems') in the Anglo-American states and France and Germany eclectically draws on poll data, literature, symbols, behaviour and institutions to explain the different emphases which the nations accord to Parsonian variables of universalism/particularism, achievement/aspiration and specificity/diffuseness.[122]

Clearly, the best method depends on the research focus. For broadly mapping a nation's political culture the survey is the most

51

appropriate; for reconstructing a past culture, content-analysis of available historical data is most suitable; for exploring the orientations of the young or the less politically aware, projective techniques are recommended.

The major challenge now facing the personality and culture approach is to provide positive accounts of the individual's and group's political psychology and culture. So far our findings have been largely negative; we know that most voters do not think along coherent or ideological lines, and that many are not very interested in or aware of politics. But to provide the positive aspects we shall have to tap the elusive and often implicit cultural assumptions. This requires us to develop, as Greenstein and Tarrow suggest, more sensitive instruments.[123] Increasingly, we may have to rely on projective and semi-projective techniques so that respondents can describe their attitudes in their own words. This does not mean, however, that other types of evidence will be rejected. The work of Karl Deutsch and his associates has been interesting for its successful adoption of a variety of vantage-points to study Franco-German integration between 1955 and 1965.[124] Among the different types of data and evidence employed were interviews with elites, content-analysis of the press, aggregate data on patterns of trade, travel and mail, and so on. Doubtless, eclecticism in the use of source-material and a willingness to appropriate insights from other disciplines will continue to be the order of the day in studying the political culture.

Because patterns of a group's political orientations only become distinctive when they differ from those of other groups, we may say that comparison is basic to the delineation of a group's political culture. For example, I have elsewhere suggested that the frequent comparison of the political societies of Britain with those of France or the United States has led to (undue) emphasis being paid to the allegiant, consensual and deferential features of the former; comparison with, say, Japan might heighten alternative aspects for Britain.[125] In comparing their five national samples, Almond and Verba were impressed by the extent to which Britain and America contained the most participant and competent citizens. However, when they later focused solely on these two cultures, they were led to define the British as a 'deferential political culture'. This was true, perhaps, as long as we confined our perspective to comparison with the United States only; the original five-nation perspective highlighted Britain as a 'participant political culture'.

Clearly, what we compare is important. Britain and America, to return to the Almond and Verba example, were more *comparable* than any other two nations in that they were roughly similar along several dimensions (stability, liberal-democracy, language, social and economic development), and this made it easier to trace the connections between the relatively fewer differing factors. In other words, broad similarities between the objects to be studied permit us to make statements like 'more or less' which are the essence of the comparative approach.[126] As Lipset noted in his study of Anglo-American political and social systems : 'Only when we know what is unique on a comparative scale can we begin to ask significant questions about causal relationships within a country.'[127]

Analysing and comparing political cultures on the basis of survey data across nations presents two immediate problems. The first is the *technical* one, involving the standardisation of questions and interview situations across the national groups, and has already been referred to. The second difficulty is a *conceptual* one of maximising the comparability of the cross-national data. Perhaps the most thorough attempt to deal with the problems of seeking equivalent indicators across nations was made in *The Civic Culture*.[128] Included among the research strategies for increasing comparability were :

1. Concentrating on the patterns of relations among variables within the nations. For example, analysis of amounts of political participation by level of education placed the differing national rates of participation in a new light. The more educated tended to participate more frequently, regardless of nation. Of course, the content of a 'high' education differed in each country. But adopting ordinal measures of education within each nation heightened the comparability.
2. Concentrating on the individual and his subjective outlook. Instead of comparing the institutions across countries, Almond and Verba compared the individual's subjective feelings towards the system.

3. Selecting the least constrained or formal activities for constructing indicators of participation, competence, and so on. For example, as an indicator of political interest, comparison of exposure to politics in the mass media between Mexico and Britain is vitiated by the much greater penetration of the media in the latter country. The greater constraints placed on party membership or voting in the United States, compared with Britain, make these features invalid indicators of political participation. On the other hand, attending campaign speeches or talking about politics are less constrained and therefore more comparable as indicators. For example, Almond and Verba measured qualitative differences among political partisans by respondents' attitudes towards elections and to the marriage of a son or daughter across party lines. Depending on their emotional involvement, according to these indicators, citizens were classified as open, apathetic, intense and parochial partisans. The typology is summarily indicated in Table 2. Our primary interest here is in the explicit use by Almond and Verba of subjective views as a means of heightening the cross-material equivalences of the indicators of partisanship.

Table 2

Typology of Partisanship by Emotional Attitudes

	Attitudes to elections	Attitudes to inter-party marriage
Open partisan	√	–
Apathetic partisan	–	–
Intense partisan	×	√
Parochial partisan	–	√

Key: – = indifference.
√ = involvement but tolerant of opponents.
× = involvement and hostile to opponents.

6. PROBLEMS AND SHORTCOMINGS

The fatal attractiveness of the political culture approach is that it may be made to explain too much. It has been used to cover so many disparate phenomena that it is easily used as a residual factor.[129] The pressing need is to break the global concept of culture into its component parts and to make it a more parsimonious tool for explanation. We examine below three examples of stereotyped views of British, French and American political cultures. These have been singled out because in each case they represent abridgements and simplifications of a complex web of orientations and have often been advanced as sweeping explanations of diverse political behaviour.

THE DEFERENTIAL ENGLISH

Elsewhere I have explored the variegated uses and misuses which political scientists have made of political and/or social deference in Britain.[130] A legion of scholars has fastened on the feature and, using differing measures and indicators of deference, made it a key explanation of such factors as working-class support for the Conservative Party, the strength and stability of British government, the monopoly of political office by men of high social status, the existence of aristocratic institutions like the monarchy and the House of Lords, etc. In many empirical studies the indicators of deference were rather weak and were poorly linked to the factors they were supposed to explain.

For example, in so far as a respondent's preference for a political leader of high social status over one of low status validly measures deference, it appears that about a fifth of British workers are deferential. However, this indicator does not tap many expected attitudes. For example, McKenzie and Silver found no association between deference and lack of political self-confidence, and Nordlinger found that his deferentials were less politically submissive than pragmatists or non-deferentials, and that they more frequently resented their low political influence than did the latter.

More serious perhaps has been the fact that an uncritical acceptance of the deference theory has dulled the sensitivity of several researchers to non-deferential political attitudes and behaviour, as well as to plausible explanations of, for example, working-class support for the Conservative Party without reference to the deference theory. We would certainly want to stress, as do Butler and Stokes, the socialisation of many children into political allegiance before Labour became a major party. A good example of the all-encompassing nature of the theory is offered in the researches of Eric Nordlinger and Robert McKenzie and Allan Silver. Nordlinger found that 58 per cent of his deferential workers thought that big business in Britain had too much power; McKenzie and Silver, however, found that only 30 per cent of their deferentials shared such a view.[131] Both studies, nevertheless, found such data to be supportive of the theory of deference. A case of 'heads I win, tails you lose', and the British are deferential regardless!

THE REVOLUTIONARY TRADITION IN FRANCE

This again, I would suggest, is a vague, amorphous and stereotyped view that is easily invoked when we discuss France's political instability, the multiplicity of political parties, the *incivisme* of the adult population, and so on. As with deference, such grand terms as 'history' or 'style' or *tendances* often redescribe what needs to be explained. Greenstein and Tarrow, in an extremely acute critique of studies of French political culture, have pointed to the highly literary and unempirical quality of such writings.[132] The conventional emphasis accorded the 'paradoxes' and 'mixes' in the culture are tantalisingly ambiguous and non-falsifiable; de Tocqueville is cited almost as a reflex action in such discussions (cf. Bagehot on evaluations of English deference), as if the writer were propounding some eternal verity. Formulae are repeated as self-evident truths and rarely refined in the light of empirical data. Remarkable sway has been exercised by notions that French society is polarised along cumulative lines

56

of cleavage which, because of the mutually reinforcing socialising agents, have cultivated among Frenchmen a set of intensely held and internally consistent attitudes. In fact, as Greenstein and Tarrow coolly observe, the evidence to support notions of the French being highly politicised and thinking along *tendance* lines is very scanty indeed. Available data suggest that the French tend to be low in levels of political information, political interest and party identification in comparison with Americans. Speculation that French support for 'flash' parties like the Poujadists derives from intense political involvement and high partisanship might be more persuasively replaced with data-based explanations of the weak attachments of Frenchmen to the established parties of the Fourth Republic. Much of our discussion about French political culture has, it seems, involved the attribution of attitudes and values held by the minority of political ideologists to the population at large. Instead of seeing the bulk of the French as being super-political, we are probably more correct in seeing them as relatively apolitical.[133]

AMERICAN POPULISM

The populist and anti-elitist aspects of American politics have often attracted 'cultural' explanations. For example, the wide grass-roots support for Senator Joseph McCarthy and his anti-communist campaign in the 1950s has been explained in these terms by such theorists of 'mass politics' as Kornhauser, Lipset, Shils and Hofstadter. According to one line of argument, McCarthy's supporters lacked group ties to the institutions of modern industrial society and rejected the progress of industrialism and urbanism as a threat to American ideals. Shils and Lipset have related McCarthyism and the populist threats to civil liberties and privacy to the lack of deference for political leaders in America.[184] Hofstadter has linked it to a 'status politics' in which anti-establishment politicians are able to attract a following among the socially marginal — among those, for example, who felt that their status had not kept pace with the rise in their incomes, or who were recent immigrants over-identifying with 'Americanism'.[185]

A careful study, drawing on sociological and survey data, has found little evidence to support these speculations about 'mass politics', 'anti-elitism' and populism.[136] Instead, Michael Rogin

57

has shrewdly pointed to the relevance of political factors by which we might explain McCarthyism, and stressed in particular the party and religious affiliations, and issue-preferences, of followers of the Senator. Rogin found that supporters tended to be (a) conservative Republicans, (b) Roman Catholics who were hostile to communism, (c) of right-wing political and economic preferences, and (d) drawn from traditional Republican areas. Given that McCarthy was an anti-communist, Republican, Roman Catholic, it is quite plausible for us to relate his popular support to the contemporary political issues, and the political and social structure.

Discussion of these stereotypes leads us to consider another unfortunate tendency of the political culture theorists, namely, their tendency to de-emphasise the influences of the political variables themselves on the system's performance. Giovanni Sartori has protested against the reductionist tendency to see party systems as reflections of socio-economic cleavages and cultural factors.[137] Instead, he has suggested that there is always an area in which political manipulation – in the case of America, for example, the single-member, simple plurality electoral system – is decisive and may translate the social and cultural influence into the party systems. Again, in comparing the stability of British political institutions with those of France, political factors would seem to be of great importance. Britain has been fortunate in that basic crises connected with salient aspects of the process of state- and nation-building have been separated, and this has lightened the load that the political system has had to face at any one time. In France, on the other hand, problems have tended to coincide. In the late nineteenth century, major problems affecting relations between church and state, the integration of the working class into the political system, and whether the state should be a monarchy or a republic, coincided. Accordingly, one may emphasise the greater stakes involved in French politics and the more acute challenge facing the elites as an explanation of her instability. We could also 'rewrite' the usual relationships between allegiance and the performance of government. The *incivisme* of French and Italian adults seems to derive from a sense of frustration at the non-responsiveness of the political institutions and a poorly developed sense of participation in the decisions of government. In Britain, there is a greater sense of trust in the government, the police and the civil service, and a feeling that all three groups will give the citizen a 'fair deal' and respond to popular demands. In these cases the actual performance of the political institutions, particularly the experience of citizens with them, appears to be a major influence on values. What we are stressing is that the culture is formed by many influences, including the political system itself, that its use as an explanatory factor should never be other than as an intervening factor, and that we should adopt a less determinist view of the political variables. Values and attitudes are undoubtedly relevant to an explanation of the performance of political systems, but eventually we have to go back and explain how the political culture came to be formed and expressed the way that it is.

More defeatist are the charges that political ideas and the political culture are not important, and that measurement of popular attitudes is of little value as they rarely manage to impress themselves on the political system. Let us examine each of these objections in turn. The first is, of course, a familiar argument of Marxists. They argue that the political culture is derivative from the social and economic structure. The dominant ideas and values in a society are those of the ruling classes, and economic control is the means of achieving an intellectual and cultural hegemony. Ideas such as constitutionalism and parliamentary democracy are a means for legitimising rule by an exploitative minority and developing a false consciousness among the exploited masses. Such an analysis of the essentially secondary importance of the political culture did not stop with Marx, however. Frank Parkin and Ralph Miliband have recently argued that major political, social and economic institutions and the values they represent result in a dominant culture or normative order which legitimises and buttresses the *status quo* in capitalist societies (see Table 3).[188] The failure of socialist parties in Western Europe to bring about radical changes in the distribution of wealth and status is, it is argued, traceable to those parties' acceptance of the dominant culture. In addition, the fact that these norms are internalised[139] by many of the non-elite, particularly the working class, serves to integrate them into the political and social system and thereby lessens the effectiveness of any challenge by non-elites. In fact, it is true that commitment to symbols of the dominant British culture, such as the public schools, the monarchy and the free-enterprise economy, is widely distributed among the British working class, including Labour voters.

Table 3

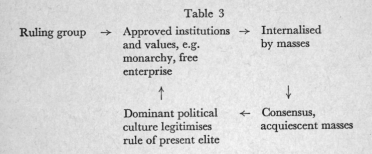

On several counts this is a very perceptive use of the tool of political culture. Parkin distinguishes the dominant political culture from other subcultures. Also, without denying the importance of the cultural factor, he considers the interests which are concerned to promote and profit from it. Finally, he succinctly suggests the inequality in the normative and legitimising resources available to conservative and socialist parties in most Western states.

On a different level is the argument that it is impossible to build up a picture of a political culture because people do not have *political* opinions or attitudes. The assumption that they do presumes a degree of political awareness and information, and an ability to connect with the political world, that empirical research, as well as everyday observations, suggest is simply not true.[140] A clear statement about the incoherent, non-systemic nature of the public's attitudes has been offered by Philip Converse in his important article, 'The Nature of Belief Systems in Mass Publics'.[141] Converse's careful and detailed sifting of surveys of mass attitudes to politics shows how frequently respondents express contradictory, unstable and unrelated views. Hardly more than a tenth of American adults possessed 'systems of beliefs', defined by Converse as 'ideas and attitudes in which the elements are bound together by some form of constraint or functional independence'. Respondents having such outlooks tended to be those of higher education and higher status. The Butler and Stokes surveys found that between 1964 and 1966 only a little over a third of British respondents retained the same views on the issues of nationalisation and nuclear weapons.[142] Wide variations between surveys are also found when interviewees are asked to appraise their political institutions or their own roles therein. For example, Almond and Verba found that large proportions of British voters thought themselves competent to influence the administration. In stark contrast with this is the finding of a recent survey that only a fifth felt that they had enough say in how the country was governed.[143] These inconsistencies suggest a reason why so many of the beliefs and values conventionally seen as part of the political culture fail to impress themselves directly on the political system. The individual lacks what Converse calls 'the contextual grasp' to relate general principles (e.g. 'there should be free speech', 'I am in favour of restraint in wage demands') to specific applications of them. For example, the citizen, while at the same time expressing the above general sentiments, is also refusing free speech to certain minorities and striking in support of his own wage demands. As a corollary, we come back to our earlier point: 'ideologies', belief-systems, 'political formulae', or generally consistent bodies of beliefs, are most likely to be the property of political elites.

More specific is the charge that study of norms, sentiments and beliefs, which are often taken for granted, is not amenable to survey methods. I am not unsympathetic to this observation, but the lesson is not that we abandon surveys but that we search around for better research instruments. There is a real shortcoming anyway with the surveys to date in that they have approached the political culture as a head-counting exercise. In reality, the political culture is almost certainly differentially determined by individuals according to their political weight and the intensity behind their particular orientations. Aggregation is only legitimate where the units to be aggregated are similar. In most cases it is the political elites, the leaders, activists and writers, who play the major role in creating and interpreting the 'political formula' of a group or nation, and their responses should be given greater weight by the researcher. Moreover, the emphasis on the individual's orientations to and participation in politics is very much a 'culture-bound' approach. Concentration on the individual is, for example, an inappropriate approach to the study of Japanese political culture where the small group is the basic social unit. Our notions of 'civic competence' apply to an individual; they are understood in Japan, however, in terms of the group. According to one writer on Japan, it is the 'individual acquiescence in group desires or their expression by leaders, rather than the Western concept of individual will or commitment' which is 'the legitimate basis of decision',[144] that is, the guide to Japanese behaviour.

A problem which may be more serious, because less obvious, is involved in the abstraction for analytical purposes of the political from the larger culture and the isolation of one aspect of the political culture. In isolation the particular feature may look different than when considered in its larger context. For example, if we focus on an individual's respect for governmental institutions and personnel as an indepedent variable, it will look very different according to whether (a) the respect is accorded regardless of the performance or responsiveness of the institutions, or (b) it follows on the responsiveness of institutions and political elites to the citizen's demands. In the first case we are dealing with a form of submissiveness which is related to a passive political outlook; in the latter case the submissiveness appears to be embedded in a more competent and positive outlook.[145]

This leads us on to the micro–macro problems of political analysis, that is, of establishing relationships between micro-units, such as the individual, and macro-units such as the electorate, the nation-state or the political party.[146] The status of these particular examples will vary according to our observational standpoint; the nation is a macro-unit from the point of view of the individual citizen, but a micro-unit when viewed as one of five groups, as in the Almond and Verba study. Psychologists, and some sociologists too, use data on individuals to explain the behaviour of groups and collectives. Almond and Verba, for example, explain the political culture of each nation in terms of the frequencies measured at the lower levels of the individuals. But reasoning by inference from the individual to the larger collectivity of which he is a part, and vice versa, or generally linking the two phenomena, may fall prey to two 'fallacies'. To assign to individuals the attributes of the larger group of which they are a part is an example of the 'ecological fallacy'. The 'individualistic fallacy' involves a causal argument from the aggregated features of individuals to the global characteristics of a group of which the individuals are members. Erwin Scheuch has pointed out that the proportion of respondents who express (to pollsters) their support of liberal-democratic values does not tell us how 'democratic' the political system is. The political structure, the weight it attaches to the views of differing respondents, and the willingness of groups to act in support of their views determine the conversion of popular views into the performance of the political system.[147] For example, it is possible for the American political system to safeguard civil liberties in spite of the fact that large numbers of the population are unfamiliar with or unsympathetic towards such principles. It is possible for the British government to get its basic policy decisions complied with in spite of the survey evidence that a majority of voters may think that it is governing badly, or unrepresentatively, or that it should resign.

Such aggregate data are also likely to be misleading as a basis for making inferences about large-scale societies whose members are undergoing differential rates of change. John Lewis has suggested that in China 'the typical' peasant or worker may simply not exist, given the variations in which Mao has managed to 'revolutionise' the political culture. According to Lewis:

> Aggregate data that may be used to identify ideal patterns lose their value for analysis of actual political orientations and attitudes. As elsewhere the modernisation of China has begun to structure these orientations and attitudes along a broad continuum and has thereby rendered meaningless those simplistic interpretations of domestic Chinese politics based on general policy pronouncements and composite data.[148]

The final difficulty centres on establishing the nature of the causal connections between the values and the performance of the political system. The difficulty here, of course, is that the two variables, of values and of political performance, are themselves both cause and consequence of other features. Empirical theories of democracy have often been plagued by imprecise hypotheses, by poor operationalisation of concepts and by not being expressed in a form amenable to proof or disproof. Brian Barry's comparative study of sociological (value-based) and economic (rationality-based) theories of democracy is especially severe on such shortcomings of the sociologists.[149] Barry's own conclusion is that the theory of economists like Mancur Olson and Anthony Downs, though imperfect at certain points, is an improvement on that of the sociologists in that they stated axioms from which deductions suitable for empirical research could be made.

ASSESSMENT

How might we assess the use which political scientists have made of the political culture approach? On the positive side, it is clear that this part of what David Easton considers the 'environment' of the political system is worth getting at, and, on the whole, many of the crudities and 'reductionism' of the 'national character' type of analysis of the immediate post-war years have been avoided. The descriptive gains are an undoubted advance on the impressionism of previous studies. On balance, the political culture approach furnishes us with more explicit, if still imperfect, tools for political analysis. It is unlikely that we shall be able to make predictions about political behaviour or even arrive at a set of testable propositions. But appreciating the subjective environment in which political action takes place and in which individuals are likely to structure and respond to situations does increase our understanding of possible political outcomes.

On the other hand, shortcomings remain. Often, it must be admitted, these derive from the formidable conceptual and technical difficulties involved in relating the political culture factors to other political phenomena. In these concluding pages we shall try to fasten on to some of these conceptual problems as they relate to some of the more widely publicised works. Given the fact that writers like Eckstein, Almond and Verba, and Nordlinger are partly concerned to fashion heuristic theories, some of the difficulties arise from the preliminary nature and incomplete testing of their theories. Basic concepts are often poorly worked out. Unhelpfully, Harry Eckstein interchanges legitimacy, effectiveness and longevity to indicate political stability in his *Theory of Stable Democracy*. Again, it is not exactly clear how democratic the government is allowed to be, for (according to Eckstein) it is supposed to be in harmony with social structures like the family and school in which relations are inevitably directive and out of tune with democratic patterns.

Turning to the civic culture theory of Almond and Verba and the related authority hypothesis of Nordlinger, we find that here also we are faced with rather awkward bases from which to derive testable hypotheses. The actual amounts of desired participation and acquiescence, and the preferred distribution of these qualities among differing groups, are not specified. The problems of measuring amounts of civic culture are also considerable. The definition of democracy in the two studies is scrupulously avoided, though the unstated assumption is that such a system is identified with the British and American political systems. The recent attempt of Deane Neubauer to compile an index of democraticness across twenty-three nations is sobering for this assumption.[150] Neubauer's index consisted of three measurable indicators designed to assess the relative amounts of electoral equality and competition across the countries. The indicators are relatively non-controversial: information equality, equality of representation, and percentage of adult population eligible to vote. The United States was ranked fifteenth on this index, behind Italy and Germany.

A further problem is that survey questions are at times inadequately addressed to some of the concepts they are supposed to tap. Nordlinger's indicator of deference, i.e. preference for a political leader of high social status over one of comparable qualifications but lacking high status, seems weak unless we also control the reasons behind the choice. A recent cross-national survey tried to measure the legitimacy of governments in the eyes of schoolchildren by asking them if they thought the government to be helpful, infallible, omniscient, etc.[151] Finding that many English children were quite detached and pragmatic in their evaluations of the government, the authors felt justified in writing of the comparatively 'low levels of support' for government. This judgement arises only from their questionable dichotomisation of criticism and support: their indicators did not allow for the posibility of *critical support*. But even when the problems of locating valid indicators for concepts have been overcome, there is the problem of interpreting the responses. Again, the literature on political culture and socialisation offers examples of where interpretations are poorly supported by the data-base. Almond and Verba and Nordlinger place interpretations on the British and English political culture which at times fly in the face of their data.

The problems associated with conceptualisation and operationalisation of the concepts lead to difficulties in linking the culture variables with the variables of political performance, institutions, stable democracy, and so on. If we establish a connection between (1) stable democracy and (2) the civic culture, or (3) a deferential political culture, or (4) congruent authority relations, then how do we establish the direction of the causal link? In the final chapter of *The Civic Culture* it is implied that the patterns of orientations found in Britain and America amount to a civic culture and that this culture accounts for the democratic stability of these two countries. In fact much of this discussion reads like a rationalisation of the data found on attitudes in these countries. All that one can say after examining the data and reading the discussion is that there is a correlation between, on the one hand, the participant-cum-allegiant values and, on the other, the British and American political systems. I am not even sure why we should regard the values as 'appropriate' or 'congruent' for such systems, other than because we have discovered them there. The actual relationship between the values and the structures is likely to be one of mutual reinforcement over time, and the fact that they interact in this way makes it wellnigh impossible to separate the values from the performance of the political structure.

Testing hypotheses about the effects on political structures of a change in values demands exacting experimental conditions, e.g. controlling for extraneous factors such as wars and economic depressions, and developing criteria for measuring and changing degrees of qualities such as civic culture and congruence at different points in time, and then waiting to see how change in one factor affects change in the other. For example, to validate ideally McClelland's theory of need-achievement as a facilitator of

66

economic development, one would need to have matched samples of children who were exposed to sets of reading which in one case emphasised high need-achievement and in the other low needs, and then wait for a generation to see if economic growth moved in the predicted direction.[152]

We need to be cautious in a number of areas. Of course, abstractions like 'the British political culture' are not very helpful. Although a major focus of the political scientist's research is still the nation-state, we must remember that national and cultural boundaries do not always coincide. In Canada many Québecois look to France and in Northern Ireland many Catholics look to Dublin for cultural identity. Or states like Yugoslavia and Soviet Russia may be composed of differing nationalities and cultures. Greater appreciation of the variations within the overall pattern is certainly in order. For example, it was the virtual ignorance of the cultural differences within the five nations that led the authors of *The Civic Culture* to present overly simple views of the respective national cultures.

Emphasising the subcultures is also a method of resolving the vexing problems of aggregation, of building up from studies of micro-phenomena to the collectivity of which they form a part. Building up from the subcultures or the level of the group is a way of bridging the gap between the macro- and micro-levels of analysis.[153] Another strategy is to control for the differential influence of the orientations of various individuals or groups. I have already stressed that political activists and elites are more likely to be related to political action and therefore more likely to be directly impressed on the political system. Robert Dahl has recently defended such a research approach along the following lines: 'This concern does not mean that the beliefs held among less influential strata are irrelevant, but only that a stronger case can be made for treating the beliefs of the politically most active and involved as an important explanatory factor.'[154]

The plea here is that the political culture is not merely the result of a census of the individuals. Aggregation of units is only valid where they are similar, and this quality is invariably absent from values. We also need to guard against the assumption that values and acts are reverse sides of the same coin. Values are not automatically translated into behaviour, and a major task facing researchers in the fields of political socialisation and culture in the future is to establish linkages between the attitudes and behaviour of individuals and then to link these in turn to the performance of the political system. These linkages need to be established and not taken for granted. On the other hand, behaviour is no foolproof guide to the values of the actor. Much depends on the opportunities available in the political structure for acting on opinions. For example, in Cuba it is suggested that many workers 'participate' in voluntary work-forces without accepting the ideas of the regime; they 'participate' in response to peer-group pressure and because there are few alternatives available to them.[155] Another example of change occurring in political behaviour without there being a change in political values is seen in Northern Ireland. Here, attitudes of Catholics and Protestants to the regime have altered little despite the *overt* displays of hostility to the regime by Catholics and the concessions and reforms made in recent years by the Unionist government.

We also need to encourage more follow-up studies. Replication is an important means of tracing changes in the culture as well as testing and refining previous research findings.[156] A dozen years after the Almond and Verba data for Britain were collected, we still cite the findings as if they were necessarily applicable to Britain in 1971. Views about French political culture based on observation of the Fourth Republic are still uncritically applied to present-day France – and this in spite of the achievement of political stability, the settlement of divisive foreign and colonial issues, the progress of industrialism, and the further penetration of the mass media.

Finally, we might also draw more self-consciously on the parapolitical influences on the political culture. This means placing more emphasis on the citizen's experiences with the political institutions and elites as well as on the values of the latter. Here, Eckstein's notion of 'adjacency' is useful.

There is something of a hiatus in the development of the political culture approach. Though we are aware of the shortcomings of the major studies, we have not advanced beyond them. We know vastly more about the citizen's beliefs, attitudes and emotions about politics than we did a decade ago. We are also more aware of the complexities governing the interactions between these orientations and the actual working of the political system. Further elucidation of the relationships between the values and the performance of the system is the next challenge facing students of political culture.

REFERENCES

1. Louis Hartz, *The Liberal Tradition in America* (New York, 1958).
2. For useful discussions of the literature on national character and political culture, see the following: Alex Inkeles and Daniel J. Levinson, 'National Character, Model Personality, and the Socio-Cultural System', in Gardner Lindzey (ed), *The Handbook of Social Psychology*, 2nd ed. (Reading, Mass., 1969) pp. 418–506; Maurice L. Farber, 'The Analysis of National Character', in N. J. Smelser and W. T. Smelser (eds.), *Personality and the Social System* (New York, 1963) pp. 80–7; Gabriel A. Almond and Sidney Verba, *The Civic Culture* (Princeton, 1963) chap. 2; and the special issue of *The Annals* (1967).
3. Roy Macridis, 'Interest Groups in Comparative Analysis', *Journal of Politics*, XXIII (1961) 40.
4. S. M. Beer and Adam Ulam, *Patterns of Government* (New York, 1958) p. 32.
5. Robert Dahl, *Political Oppositions in Western Democracies* (New Haven, 1966) pp. 352–5.
6. Lucian Pye, *Politics, Personality and Nation-Building* (New Haven, 1962) pp. 122–4.
7. S. E. Finer, *The Man on Horseback* (London, 1962) chaps 7–9.
8. G. A. Almond, 'Comparative Political Systems', *Journal of Politics*, XVIII (1956).
9. Talcott Parsons and Edward Shils, *Toward a General Theory of Action* (New York, 1962) pp. 55 ff.
10. Sidney Verba, 'Germany: The Remaking of a Political Culture', in Lucian Pye and Sidney Verba, *Political Culture and Political Development* (Princeton, 1965).
11. Almond and Verba, *The Civic Culture*, pp. 17 ff.
12. Cf. Harve Mossawir, 'The Significance of an Election', M.A. thesis (University of Manchester, 1965).
13. Verba, in Pye and Verba, *Political Culture and Political Development*, pp. 131–2.

14. Max Weber, *The Protestant Ethic and the Spirit of Capitalism* (New York, 1958) p. 90.
15. G. A. Almond and G. Bingham Powell, Jr, *Comparative Politics: A Developmental Approach* (Boston, 1966) p. 50.
16. Richard Fagen, *The Transformation of Political Culture in Cuba* (Stanford, 1969) p. 5.
17. Reprinted in H. H. Eckstein, *Division and Cohesion in Democracy* (Princeton, 1966).
18. Finer, *The Man on Horseback*.
19. David McClelland, *The Achieving Society* (Princeton, 1961) and 'National Character and Economic Growth in Turkey and Iran', in Lucian Pye (ed.), *Communications and Political Development* (Princeton, 1963).
20. Daniel Lerner, *The Passing of Traditional Society* (Glencoe, Ill., 1958).
21. Pye, *Politics, Personality and Nation-Building*, pp. 54–5.
22. Peter Nettl, *Political Mobilisation* (London, 1967) p. 57.
23. Eric A. Nordlinger, *The Working Class Tories* (London, 1967) p. 49.
24. See the same author's 'Democratic Stability and Instability: The French Case', *World Politics*, xviii (1965).
25. Cf. Michael Crozier, *The Bureaucratic Phenomenon* (Chicago, 1964) pp. 220 ff.
26. Nicholas Wahl, 'The French Political System', in Beer and Ulam, *Patterns of Government*.
27. Eckstein, *A Theory of Stable Democracy* (see note 17 above).
28. Heinz Eulau, *The Behavioral Persuasion in Politics* (New York, 1963) p. 79.
29. J. W. Prothro and C. M. Grigg, 'Fundamental Principles of Democracy', *Journal of Politics*, xxii (1960); Herbert McClosky, 'Consensus and Ideology in American Politics', *American Political Science Review*, lviii (1964).
30. W. H. Wriggins, *Ceylon: The Dilemmas of a New Nation* (Princeton, 1960) pp. 29–33.
31. Myron Weiner, in Pye and Verba, *Political Culture and Political Development*.
32. Stanley Hoffmann, 'Heroic Leadership: The Case of Modern France', in Lewis Edinger (ed.), *Political Leadership in Industrial Societies* (New York, 1967).
33. Nathan Leites, *On the Political Game in France* (Stanford, 1959); Constantin Melnik and Nathan Leites, *The House without Windows* (Evanston, Ill., 1958).

34. Pye, *Politics, Personality and Nation-Building*.
35. See David Apter, *The Politics of Modernisation* (Chicago, 1965) chap. 6.
36. Philip Converse, 'The Nature of Belief Systems in Mass Publics', in David Apter (ed.), *Ideology and Discontent* (New York, 1964).
37. For Britain, see Nordlinger, *The Working Class Tories*.
38. Almond and Verba, *The Civic Culture*.
39. Verba, in Pye and Verba, *Political Culture and Political Development*, p. 530.
40. Joseph LaPalombara, in Pye and Verba, ibid.
41. G. A. Almond, 'Comparative Political Systems' (see note 8 above).
42. Cf. S. M. Lipset, *Political Man* (New York, 1960).
43. Arend Lijphart, *The Politics of Accommodation: Pluralism and Democracy in the Netherlands* (Berkeley, 1968).
44. Arend Lijphart, 'Consociational Democracy', *World Politics*, xxi (1969).
45. Arend Lijphart, 'Typologies of Democratic Systems', *Comparative Political Studies*, i (1968) esp. pp. 35 ff.
46. S. M. Lipset and Stein Rokkan, Introduction to *Party Systems and Voter Alignments* (New York, 1967).
47. Richard Rose and Derek Urwin, 'Social Cohesion, Political Parties and Strains in Regimes', *Comparative Political Studies*, ii (1969).
48. Derek Urwin, 'Social Changes and Political Parties in Belgium: Problems of Institutionalisation', *Political Studies*, xviii (1970).
49. Val Lorwin, 'Belgium: Religion, Class and Language in National Politics', in Dahl, *Political Oppositions in Western Democracies*, p. 174.
50. David Easton and Jack Dennis note: 'We need a more comprehensive conception of the relevance of socialisation for the political system, one in which change is not interpreted as a failure of the system to reproduce itself but is viewed positively' (*Children in the Political System* (New York, 1969) p. 42).
51. Alex Inkeles, 'Social Change and Social Character: The Role of Parental Mediation', *Journal of Social Issues*, ii (1955).
52. Verba, in Pye and Verba, *Political Culture and Political Development*.
53. For a bold and, to my mind, naïve attempt to do this for British schoolchildren, see Jack Dennis *et al.*, 'Support for Nation and Government among English Schoolchildren', *British Journal of Political Science*, i (1971).

54. On this point see Fred Greenstein, *Personality and Politics* (Chicago, 1969) p. 127.

55. On this see Fred Greenstein and Sidney Tarrow, 'The Study of French Political Socialisation', *World Politics*, xxii (1969).

56. See Dennis *et al.*, op. cit., and Ted Tapper, 'Secondary School Adolescents', Ph.D. thesis (University of Manchester, 1968).

57. See Herbert Hyman, *Political Socialisation* (New York, 1959). But cf. M. Kent Jennings and Robert G. Niemi, 'The Transmission of Political Values from Parent to Child', *American Political Science Review*, lxii (1968).

58. For studies placing major emphasis on the school, see Easton and Dennis, *Children in the Political System*, and Robert Hess and Judith Torney, *The Development of Political Attitudes in Children* (Chicago, 1967).

59. Almond and Verba, *The Civic Culture*, chap. 12.

60. Verba, in Pye and Verba, *Political Culture and Political Development*.

61. Jean Grossholtz, *Politics in the Philippines* (Boston, 1964) chap. 7.

62. Joseph LaPalombara, in Pye and Verba, *Political Culture and Political Development*, chap. 8.

63. Almond and Verba, *The Civic Culture*, chap. 10.

64. Gordon di Renzo, *Personality, Power and Politics* (Notre Dame, Ind., 1968).

65. Cf. Richard Rose, in Pye and Verba, *Political Culture and Political Development*, p. 104.

66. Guenther Roth, *The Social Democrats in Imperial Germany* (Ottawa, 1963).

67. Otto Kirchheimer, 'The Transformation of the Western European Party Systems', in Joseph LaPalombara and Myron Weiner (eds), *Political Parties and Political Development* (Princeton, 1965).

68. Dahl, *Political Oppositions in Western Democracies*.

69. Apter, *The Politics of Modernisation*, p. 210.

70. LaPalombara and Weiner, *Political Parties and Political Development*, pp. 424–7.

71. See Paul Abramson *et al.*, 'The Development of Systematic Support in Four Western Democracies', *Comparative Political Studies*, ii (1970).

72. Edward Shils, *The Torment of Secrecy* (London, 1957) p. 48; Harry Eckstein, 'The British Political System', in Beer and Ulam, *Patterns of Government*, pp. 78 ff.

73. Almond and Verba, *The Civic Culture*, p. 503.

74. Maurice Zeitlin, *Revolutionary Politics and the Cuban Working Class* (Princeton, 1967).

75. 'To most of the citizens of the West the currently active parties have been part of the political landscape since their childhood' (Lipset and Rokkan, *Party Systems and Voter Alignments*, p. 50).
76. Richard Rose, *Governing without Consensus: An Irish Perspective* (London, 1971).
77. For samples of this approach see Hans Daalder, in Pye and Verba, *Political Culture and Political Development*, chap. 2, and Stanley Rothman, 'Modernity and Tradition in Britain', reprinted in Richard Rose (ed.), *Studies in British Politics*, 2nd ed. (London, 1969).
78. L. W. Wylie, *Village in the Vaucluse* (Cambridge, Mass., 1957).
79. Grossholtz, *Politics in the Philippines*.
80. Richard Rose, *Politics in England* (London, 1965) p. 79; Harry Eckstein, 'Authority Relations and Governmental Performance', *Comparative Political Studies*, II (1969) 304.
81. See sources cited in my 'The Deferential English: A Comparative Critique', *Government and Opposition*, VI 3 (1971).
82. Robert Scott, in Pye and Verba, *Political Culture and Political Development*.
83. See the country studies in Pye and Verba, ibid.
84. See my discussion about micro–macro problems, pp. 62–3 below, and also S. M. Lipset and Reinhard Bendix, *Social Mobility in Industrial Society* (Berkeley, 1959).
85. Frank Myers, 'Social Class and Political Change in Western Industrial Systems', *Comparative Politics*, II 3 (1970).
86. Robert Lane, *Political Ideology* (New York, 1962).
87. Myers, op. cit., p. 394.
88. See the contributions by Rose and Ward in Pye and Verba, *Political Culture and Political Development*.
89. Rajni Kothari, 'Tradition and Modernity Revisited', *Government and Opposition*, III 3 (1968).
90. Cf. Frank Langdon, *Politics in Japan* (Boston, 1967) pp. 74–5.
91. Cf. Robert Packenham, 'Development Doctrines in Foreign Aid', *World Politics*, XVIII (1966).
92. This is not dissimilar to Karl Deutsch's definition of social mobilisation, viz. 'the process in which major cultures are eroded and broken down, and people become available for new patterns of socialisation and behaviour'. See his 'Social Mobilisation and Political Development', *American Political Science Review*, LV (1961).

93. Alex Inkeles, 'Participant Citizenship in Six Developing Countries', *American Political Science Review*, LXIII (1969).
94. S. M. Lipset, 'Some Social Requisites of Democracy', *American Political Science Review*, LIII (1959).
95. P. Cutright, 'National Political Development: Measurement and Analysis', *American Sociological Review*, XXVIII (1963). Cutright actually states that political development is 'interdependent' with such factors as education, labour-force distribution, the communications system, urbanisation and economic development (ibid., p. 255).
96. Deane Neubauer, 'Some Conditions of Democracy', *American Political Science Review*, LXI (1967).
97. Pye (ed.), *Communications and Political Development*, p. 125.
98. F. T. C. Yu, ibid. Research on the impact of the mass media on political attitudes in the West has suggested that they have only a modest effect. Whether or not such a judgement should apply to the explicit efforts to mould outlooks in more totalitarian societies is doubtful.
99. Apter, *The Politics of Modernisation*, p. 366.
100. Ibid.
101. Fagen, *The Transformation of Political Culture in Cuba*, p. 15.
102. Yu, in Pye (ed.), *Communications and Political Development*, p. 264. See also James Townsend, *Political Participation in Communist China* (Berkeley, 1966).
103. Louis Hartz, *The Founding of New Societies* (New York, 1964).
104. Almond and Verba, *The Civic Culture*.
105. Almond, 'Comparative Political Systems' (see note 8 above).
106. Almond and Verba, *The Civic Culture*.
107. Cf. Richard Rose, 'Modern Nations and the Study of Political Modernisation', in Stein Rokkan (ed.), *Comparative Research across Cultures and Nations* (The Hague, 1968) chap. 7.
108. Almond and Verba, *The Civic Culture*, pp. 338–41.
109. Robert McKenzie and Allan Silver, *Angels in Marble* (London, 1968).
110. David Butler and Donald Stokes, *Political Change in Britain* (London, 1969).
111. Scott, in Pye and Verba, *Political Culture and Political Development*, pp. 335, 345 ff.
112. A. H. Brown, 'Political Change in Czechoslovakia', *Government and Opposition*, IV 2 (1969).
113. Robert Lane, 'The Politics of Consensus in an Age of Affluence', *American Political Science Review*, LIX (1965).

114. Almond and Verba, *The Civic Culture*, p. 43.
115. Cf. A. L. George, 'The Problem of Circularity in Using a Person's Beliefs to Explain His Behaviour', mimeo (Stanford, 1968).
116. For example, the response rates for the Almond and Verba study varied from 59 per cent for the British sample to 80 per cent for the American. The Italian sample located only 10 per cent of socialist and communist voters, though one-third of the electorate voted for these parties.
117. See Almond and Verba, *The Civic Culture*, chap. 2, and Stein Rokkan and Sidney Verba, *Comparative Survey Analysis* (The Hague, 1969).
118. Fagen, *The Transformation of Political Culture in Cuba*.
119. Nathan Leites, *A Study of Bolshevism* (Glencoe, Ill., 1953).
120. New York, 1962.
121. Indicators of achievement-needs were references to the need to perform tasks competently, finding new methods for solving problems, and getting ahead in life.
122. S. M. Lipset, *The First New Nation* (London, 1964) pp. 16–18.
123. Greenstein and Tarrow, 'The Study of French Political Socialisation' (see note 55 above) esp. p. 133.
124. Karl Deutsch *et al.*, *France, Germany and the Western Alliance* (New York, 1967).
125. Kavanagh, 'The Deferential English', p. 356 (see note 81 above).
126. A. L. Kalleberg, 'The Logic of Comparison', *World Politics*, XVIII (1965).
127. S. M. Lipset, 'Anglo-American Society', *International Encyclopedia of Social Science* (New York, 1967) p. 401.
128. Almond and Verba, *The Civic Culture*, pp. 68–72.
129. Cf. Fred Greenstein's explicit avoidance of the term in his *Personality and Politics*, p. ix.
130. Kavanagh, 'The Deferential English'.
131. Nordlinger, *The Working Class Tories*, p. 109; McKenzie and Silver, *Angels in Marble*, p. 208.
132. Greenstein and Tarrow, 'The Study of French Political Socialisation'.
133. Philip Converse and George Dupeux, 'Politicisation of the Electorate in France and the United States', *Public Opinion Quarterly*, XXVI (1962) 1–23.
134. Lipset, *The First New Nation*, p. 252; Shils, *The Torment of Secrecy*.
135. Richard Hofstadter, 'The Pseudo-Conservative Revolt', in Daniel Bell (ed.), *The New American Right* (New York, 1955).

136. Michael P. Rogin, *McCarthy and the Intellectuals: The Radical Specter* (Cambridge, Mass., 1967) chaps 1–2.
137. Giovanni Sartori, 'Sociology of Politics and Politics of Sociology', *Government and Opposition*, IV 2 (1969).
138. Frank Parkin, *Middle Class Radicalism* (Manchester, 1968) pp. 22–3; Ralph Miliband, *Parliamentary Socialism* (London, 1961).
139. Note that acceptance of the dominant culture is not necessarily due to brainwashing.
140. For a bold statement of this view, see Bernard Hennessy, 'A Headnote on the Existence and Study of Political Attitudes', *Social Science Quarterly*, LI (1970).
141. In Apter (ed.), *Ideology and Discontent*.
142. Butler and Stokes, *Political Change in Britain*, pp. 178 ff.
143. Richard Rose and Harve Mossawir, 'Voting and Elections', *Political Studies*, XV (1967).
144. Langdon, *Politics in Japan*, p. 203.
145. I think this is true of the concept of deference as handled by Nordlinger and by McKenzie and Silver.
146. For useful discussions on this, see Eulau, *The Behavioral Persuasion in Politics*, pp. 123–7; Greenstein, *Personality and Politics*, chap. 5; and contributions in Mattei Dogan and Stein Rokkan (eds), *Quantitative Ecological Analysis in the Social Sciences* (Cambridge, Mass., 1968).
147. Erwin K. Scheuch, 'Cross-National Comparisons Using Aggregate Data', in R. L. Merritt and Stein Rokkan, *Comparing Nations* (New Haven, 1968).
148. John Lewis, 'The Study of Chinese Political Culture', *World Politics*, XVIII (1966) 524.
149. Brian Barry, *Sociologists, Economists and Democracy* (London, 1970).
150. Neubauer, op. cit. (see note 96 above).
151. See Dennis *et al.*, op. cit. (note 53 above).
152. Irving Louis Horowitz, 'Dimensions in Comparative International Development', *Social Science Quarterly*, LI (1970) 509.
153. For a persuasive criticism of the whole systems approach and an appeal for the segmented approach, see Joseph LaPalombara, 'Parsimony and Empiricism in Comparative Politics: An Anti-Scholastic View', in Robert T. Holt and John E. Turner (eds), *The Methodology of Comparative Research* (New York, 1970) chap. 4.
154. Robert Dahl, *Polyarchy* (New York, 1971) p. 127.

155. Fagen, *The Transformation of Political Culture in Cuba*, p. 152. I have placed 'participation' in quotes to suggest that it is coerced.
156. LaPalombara speaks of 'indiscriminate fishing expeditions for data' ('Parsimony and Empiricism . . .', p. 138).

SELECT BIBLIOGRAPHY

This essay has already reviewed many of the salient works in the field of political culture and there is little point in going over similar ground. Instead, it is proposed to mention a dozen or so useful texts for the student who wishes to come to grips with major aspects of the subject. I have frequently referred to *The Civic Culture* by Gabriel A. Almond and Sidney Verba (Princeton, 1963), and this is essential reading not only for students of political culture but also for those concerned with problems of comparative research. The volume *Political Culture and Political Development*, edited by Lucian Pye and Sidney Verba (Princeton, 1965), contains several interesting country studies by specialist authors as well as stimulating keynote and concluding chapters by the editors. Also recommended are Gabriel Almond's 'Comparative Political Systems' (*Journal of Politics*, xviii, 1956) – perhaps the earliest attempt to apply the political culture approach to the study of government – and chap. 2 of Richard Rose's *People in Politics* (London, 1970), an incisive piece of synthesis. Seymour Lipset's *Political Man* (New York, 1960) has been influential and, in spite of occasional sloppiness, is still worth reading.

Political Socialisation by Richard E. Dawson and Kenneth Prewitt (Boston, 1969) is a useful introduction to the subject. The article 'The Study of French Political Socialisation' (*World Politics*, xxii, 1969) by Fred Greenstein and Sidney Tarrow is also useful as a corrective to some of the more sweeping claims advanced on behalf of study of the political orientations of children, and statements about the French political culture. On the conceptual and methodological problems involved in linking personality and values to political phenomena, Brian Barry's *Sociologists, Economists and Democracy* (London, 1970), and Fred Greenstein's *Personality and Politics* (Chicago, 1969), are both excellent. For an explicit attempt to relate one aspect of the political culture to democratic stability, see Harry Eckstein's *A Theory of Stable Democracy,* reprinted in his *Division and Cohesion in Democracy* (Princeton, 1966). Studies of English political and social deference offer some interesting information as well as illustrating many of the more glaring shortcomings of the political culture approach. Eric Nordlinger's *The Working Class Tories* (London, 1967), and *Angels in Marble* by Robert McKenzie and Allan Silver (London, 1968), are cases in point.